THE Gold Book
OF LESSON PLANS
Volume One

TEACH
MAGAZINE • LE PROF

TEACH Magazine is dedicated to providing teachers with pragmatic tools and resources for classroom use. We have spent over 21 years developing curriculum-connected materials covering a wide range of topics and themes.

© TEACH Magazine 2014

Created in Canada

While extensive effort has gone into ensuring the reliability of the information in this book, the publisher makes no warranty, express or implied, with respect to the material contained herein.

ISBN: 978-09879018-6-6

Book fonts: Cicle and Century Schoolbook
Design by Kat Kozbiel

CONTENTS

PREFACE   iii

LESSON PLANS

LESSON ONE: Food for Thought   1
Exploring the history of agriculture and food safety

LESSON TWO: Future Worlds   21
Imagining the structure and organization of future societies

LESSON THREE: Interplanetary Citizenship   33
Citizenship of the universe comes with both rights and responsibilities

LESSON FOUR: Roll-a-Coin Through the Curriculum   43
Exploring significant people, places and events through the evolution of Canadian currency

LESSON FIVE: Star Trek   93
What the popular sci-fi series offers on lessons in morality

LESSON SIX: Stellar Arts   101
How the universe has inspired creativity over millennia

LESSON SEVEN: The Human Rights Project   109
Exploring the concepts of justice and equality in the world today

PREFACE

TEACH Magazine's dedicated staff of editors has poured over a myriad of lesson plans and identified those that have resonance and the ability to serve the needs of your students. They have been dusted off and polished up; all the elements updated are ready-to-go.

We are presenting an impressive range of themes covered within the lesson plans that appear in this book. Themes such as global citizenship, human rights, democracy, food safety, the solar system and creativity, intergalactic citizenship, societies of the future and the moral lessons of Star Trek.

You will find that the lessons are categorized by theme and grade level to facilitate simple navigation back and forth. Our wish is for you, the reader and user to find what you need quickly and easily.

We know that teachers make do and even excel with what they have on hand; that resources can be scarce as well as expensive. TEACH Magazine is focused on accessibility and disseminating the learning resources we create as widely as possible.

This book is filled with substantive content. Based on pilot testing over the years, we also know that students want to have fun while they are learning. They want to be challenged and engaged. They want to know their voices are being heard and their viewpoints count for something. These are incentives for students to do their very best work no matter the theme or idea.

We at TEACH Magazine are confident we can help you, the classroom teacher, develop or enhance that stimulus for you students. They will have fun and they will challenge and be challenged as you work your way through each of the lesson plans contained in The Gold Book before you.

We are always open to feedback and insights that you may have.

Please feel free to contact us at any time: info@teachmag.com

Enjoy the lesson plans we have provided.

Sincerely,

Wili Liberman, Editor

LESSON ONE

FOOD FOR THOUGHT:
UNDERSTANDING FOOD SAFETY AND CROP PROTECTION

The purpose of this teaching resource is to introduce the concept of crop protection to students. Students will discover that farmers employ many different methods and techniques to protect the crops they grow. Some of these methods include: crop rotation, scouting, specially breeding plants and crops that are bug and disease resistant, and the careful use of pesticides, herbicides, and fungicides.

GRADE LEVEL:
3 – 6

CURRICULA THEMES:

Science, Social Studies, Language Arts, Geography, Visual Arts, Health

INTRODUCTION

Did you know that a gigantic battle takes place every day in fields and farms across Canada? And every day Canadians go to the local market or grocery store and expect to find wholesome, nutritious food for them to buy. What happens before the food finds its way into our homes? How do we know it is safe to eat? Canada has one of the most strictly regulated and enforced agricultural systems in the world where food safety is the number one priority.

Who is fighting this battle on behalf of Canadians? You might say that the farmer is our first line of defence against bugs that damage and destroy crops, diseases that do the same, and other plants that try to take over the same territory as the plants that produce the fruits, vegetables and grains planted in fields and orchards. And then, of course, there is the weather. Farmers and growers need more than just a little bit of luck when it comes to the best possible conditions to raise healthy, robust crops.

Here are some of the foes the farmer must defeat:

Insects: When enough of them get together, they can cause serious damage to food crops, usually by chewing or sucking on various parts of the plant.

Weeds: These attack plants and are often hardier than crop plants or come up earlier in the season. Weeds inhibit the crop plant's development by competing for sunlight, space, and soil nutrients.

Fungi: They cause disease conditions in crop plants. Fungal spores germinate and grow in the right weather conditions. The fungus then becomes a parasite in the plant tissue and can kill or severely deform plant growth.

LEARNING OUTCOMES

Students will:
- Understand the history of farming and agriculture in Canada
- Gain an appreciation for the role that farmers play in providing the country with safe and nutritious food to eat
- See how food gets from the farm to the table
- Understand how crop protection techniques including the application of chemicals to fight pests and diseases affect crop yields and the quality of food products
- Acquire knowledge concerning land use, water use, and the role of nutrients in the Earth's soil
- Grow their own plant in class
- Learn about challenges facing a Canadian fruit crop: apples

- Learn to distinguish between good bugs and bad bugs
- Visit a farm to apply what they have learned
- Use critical thinking and assessment skills and techniques
- Work in teams to achieve a result

GENERAL LEARNING OUTCOMES

Science, Technology, Society and the Environment

By the end of Grade 6, it is expected that students will:
- Demonstrate that science and technology use specific processes to investigate the natural and constructed world or to seek solutions to practical problems
- Demonstrate that science and technology develop over time
- Describe ways that science and technology work together in investigating questions and problems and in meeting specific needs
- Describe the applications of science and technology that have developed in response to human and environmental needs
- Describe the positive and negative effects that result from applications of science and technology in their own lives, the lives of others, and the environment

Skills

By the end of Grade 6, it is expected that students will:
- Ask questions about objects and events in the local environment and develop plans to investigate those questions
- Observe and investigate their environment and record the results
- Interpret findings from investigations using appropriate methods
- Work collaboratively to carry out science-related activities, and communicate ideas, procedures, and results

Knowledge

By the end of Grade 6, it is expected that students will:
- Describe and compare characteristics and properties of living things, objects, and materials
- Describe and predict causes, effects, and patterns related to change in living and non-living things
- Describe interactions within natural systems and the elements required to maintain these systems

SPECIFIC LEARNING OUTCOMES

Grade 3: Earth and Space Science

Illustrative Example:

Students soon discover that there is more to soil than just dirt. It is stuff for creatures to live in and for plants to grow in, and provides a base for gardens, forests, fields, and farms. By examining soils, students discover that soils are made up of more than one thing, and that the particular combination of materials in soil has a lot to do with what lives in it and on it. By focusing on the ways we can change soil—especially changes that occur as a result of water—students learn that soil is affected by humans and the environment.

Exploration

Students examine soils for living and non-living things
- Students examine and describe a soil and its components, using magnifying glasses to observe and sieves to separate different components
- Students spread a soil sample on a white sheet of plastic and observe what crawls out of and through the soil

The above exploration may lead to the following questions: What do we find in soil/ How does soil change when it is wet?

Development

Students investigate the characteristics of soils and soil components
- Students examine different soils from the local area and describe their characteristics
- Students investigate what happens when soil gets wet: Does it feel different? Pile up differently? Hold together differently?
- Students investigate what happens when soil is shaken in a container of water

Application

- Students prepare and maintain soils
- Students make a soil from different components
- Students select and maintain the soil for growing a plant

BACKGROUND INFORMATION

History of Agriculture (*www.thecanadianencyclopedia.com/en/article/history-of-agriculture*)

Agriculture began long ago when wild animals were first domesticated. Humans became the keepers of animals, responsible for their welfare, shelter, food, and water. Humans also provided pasture for the animals and harvested and stored fodder to feed them during the winter.

Archaeological evidence shows that, as early as 2,000 years ago, Indigenous people had established successful agricultural practices. Their crops included maize (corn), beans, and squash. Some native communities developed advanced irrigation systems to provide water for their crops. When Europeans arrived, they found native people of the St. Lawrence and Great Lakes region cultivating crops and using seeds. Surplus produce was traded for skins and meat provided by hunting tribes of the region. Later, this native agriculture provided food for European fur traders, missionaries, and soldiers.

Early European agriculture in Canada consisted of little more than gardens tended within trading forts and missions. The first real farming settlement was established in 1606 at the French trading post of Port Royal in Acadia (Nova Scotia). As more French settlers arrived, they brought livestock and seed and their agricultural practices. They tamed the marshlands of the Annapolis Valley by building dykes. They tilled the land by hand, using shovels, hoes, and rakes. Seed was spread by hand from the pocket of a large apron. Crops were harvested by scythe or sickle. Grain was threshed with a hand-held flail or by being trampled underfoot by oxen that walked in circles around a fixed post.

In the St. Lawrence region, the first farm started in 1617 at the fur-trading post of Quebec. It took eight years to cultivate the first six hectares. The French government encouraged settlers to come, and by the 1640s, the colony was self-sufficient in its food production although it was an ongoing struggle.

Agriculture in what is now Ontario was dominated in the early 1800s by wheat production. Wheat was the crop most easily grown and marketed, and was an important source of cash for settlers. Apart from limited internal demand from such sources as British garrisons, canal construction crews, and lumber camps, the principal markets were Britain and Lower Canada. Technological developments assisted both the grain and livestock sectors in the 19th century. Field tillage was improved by the introduction of copies of American cast-iron plows after 1815. To control weeds, biennial summer fallow was generally practiced between about 1830 and 1850, when crop rotation became prevalent.

Agriculture in Western Canada began in earnest after 1870, when the federal government bought the former HBC territories, which included the Prairies. In 1872 the government passed the Dominion Lands Act, which established homestead rights for new settlers and set in motion the orderly survey of all the area west of the Great Lakes. The government also promised financial assistance and gifts of land to individuals and companies in return for promoting settlement. Completion of the Canadian Pacific Railway in 1885 provided a link between

Eastern and Western Canada. All this led to farms being started throughout the prairies, with a massive influx of settlers in the late 1890s and early 1900s.

The settlers of the late 19th century used oxen, horses, and sometimes steam engines to break the prairie sod. Once the sod was broken, horses provided the major source of farm power. Wheat was the chief grain crop, and the West quickly became Canada's breadbasket. The steam engine, pulling 16-furrow ploughs and powering huge threshing machines, revolutionized agriculture on the Prairies in the period from 1900 to 1920. Cattle ranching spread on grasslands that were considered unsuitable for cultivation because of climate or topography. The First World War brought a temporary boom to agriculture, which helped to finance the purchase of more machinery. But the boom waned after 1920, and by 1929 the entire world was gripped in an economic slump, the Great Depression. On the Prairies, the economic woes were made worse by the great drought of 1929 to 1937. So vast was the affected area, and so persistent the strong winds and lack of moisture, that clouds of prairie dust were reported to darken the skies as far away as New York City. As if this was not enough, the Prairies during these years were plagued by hordes of grasshoppers and by marching legions of army caterpillars.

The Second World War erupted shortly after the close of this dismal period. Once again there was a boom in prices, and once again young men left the farm to join the armed forces. Because of the preceding drought and depression, few farmers could afford to buy new tractors and other new machinery. The labour shortage continued after the war, for many of the returning servicemen did not go back to farming. To replace this lost labour force, costly new machinery was needed, so farms were consolidated into larger units so that they could afford the mechanization. The direct result was that fewer people were involved in agriculture. Today, less than 4 per cent of the Canadian population is engaged in farming, compared with more than 33 per cent in 1931.

Some of the new technologies spawned by the Second World War have found a place in the farming industry. These include herbicides and pesticides. Other developments that have helped increase production include the widespread use of chemical fertilizers; the continual genetic upgrading of plant and animal resources, made possible by research; new technologies for seeding (to conserve moisture); and harvesting (to minimize losses in quantity or quality of product).

In the late 19th and early 20th centuries, urbanization expanded the demand for market gardening around cities and more specialized crops in different regions. Dairying developed on the fringes of cities and cash crop acreages declined in favour of feed grains and fodder, while beef producers were unable to meet the domestic demand. Farm-initiated associations began to appear including stockbreeders, dairy people, grain growers, fruit growers, etc., as well as the government-initiated Farmers' Institutes and Women's Institutes.

ACTIVITY ONE
Teacher-led Discussion
(half to a full period)

Direct students to conduct research on the "history of agriculture" and see what they can find. For younger students, the teacher may want to do the search and print out the materials, which can then be handed out to the class for students to read or prepare a summary of information instead.

What are students' impressions of farming many years ago? Do they think it was a hard life and if so, why? What sorts of challenges did farmers face? And how did the farmers of the time meet those challenges? What tools did early farmers have available to them, if any?

After the discussion has ended, have students write a short paragraph about early farming life. Students may select a time period based on what they have read on the Canadian Encyclopedia website. Make sure that whatever students write is in their own words.

ACTIVITY TWO
Technology Timeline

Following is a brief overview describing technological developments for the agriculture industry:

1700 — Jethro Tull of England invented the seed drill or planter. It freed farm workers from hours of back-breaking labour.

Early 1700s — For years, farmers knew that planting the same crop in the same field each year was not a good idea. Charles "Turnip" Townshend discovered the four-crop system of crop rotation. In the first year, a farmer planted clover. In the second and third years, the farmer planted wheat. In the fourth year, the farmer planted turnips. Townshend thought turnips gave the soil many nutrients the other crops took away. (Actually, it was the clover.) This allowed farmers to raise enough forage to feed animals, allowing them to produce fresh meat throughout the year.

1831 — Cyrus McCormick invented the mechanical reaper which combined all the steps that earlier harvesting machines had performed separately. It freed farm workers from back-breaking labour.

1837 — John Deere began manufacturing steel plows, made of cast iron and wood.

1850 — It required 75-90 hours of labour to produce 40 bushels per acre of corn.

1860s — Steam power came into use on large farms. As a result, fewer farm workers were needed to produce food crops and each farm worker could produce more food to feed more people.

1880s — Bordeaux mixture (fungicide) discovered in France and soon used in North America.

1900 — It required about 35-40 hours of labour to produce 100 bushels of corn. Yields were about 40 bushels an acre.

1904 — First serious stem-rust epidemic affecting wheat.

1900-1920 — Extensive experimental work was carried out to breed disease-resistant varieties of plants, to improve plant yield and quality, and to increase the productivity of farm animal strains.

1940s — Increased use of herbicides and pesticides as a method to protect crops from diseases and insects.

1950 — It required about 10-14 hours of labour to produce 100 bushels of corn. Yields were about 50 bushels an acre. For the first time, there were more tractors on farms than work horses and mules.

1960 — Farmers moved from horsepower to tractor power. From 1940-1960, 12 million horses and mules gave way to 5 million tractors.

1960s — The modern grain drill was invented. It could plant a crop, put fertilizer in the ground, and provide for weed control all in one pass over the field. This was one of the specialized machines that allowed farmers to put the right amount of fertilizer in the right place and to count out, space, and plant just the right number of seeds for a row.

1990 — It required 2½ hours of labour to produce 100 bushels of corn. Improved seeds and better methods of controlling pests meant that yields were about 100 bushels per acre. Farmers used bio-control for pest management. For example, scientists learned that a species of ladybug would eat aphids that destroyed potato crops.

1994 — Farmers began to use satellite technology to track and plan their farming practices.

2000s — Farmers began to introduce sustainability practices, both envoronmentally and economically.

The teacher will divide students into groups of three and four and each group will select a period and conduct further Internet or library-based research concerning the period and the specific technological development. If students select a period where a farm tool or machine was developed, they may present a detailed sketch and description of how the tool or implement was used and how it made the farmer's life easier. Otherwise, all of the groups will make a short (5-6 minute) presentation on their findings. The presentations should focus on how the development was beneficial to the farmer and made it easier to do his work.

ACTIVITY THREE
Teacher-led Discussion
(half period)

Having reviewed the above timeline with the class, begin a discussion exploring the impact of technology on agricultural practices. What development from the above list do students think is the most important? Have students make their suggestions and give their reasons why they think so. At the end of the discussion, you may wish to have a vote on the subject to determine what the majority of the class thinks.

But it's not just farmers who use technology to improve how crops grow. The Canadian Space Agency was involved in the launch of a satellite called CloudSat. This satellite is capable of reading data through thermal cloud cover. It has long been thought that clouds and cloud patterns have a significant impact on weather. Until this satellite was developed, there hasn't been an accurate way of measuring the impact of cloud cover on weather patterns. Once again, technology plays a role in providing the agricultural community with better information that will help in the preparation and protection of crops.

ACTIVITY FOUR
Background Information: In the Field

A seed is placed in a warm, moist environment and it begins to grow. The first root emerges from the root's embryo and grows downward to form a root system. A shoot grows upward to form the stem, leaves, and flowers. The plant then draws water and elements from the soil like a straw. Molecules of water and nutrients enter the roots, travel up the stem and throughout the plant. Tiny openings called "stomata" on the leaf surface allow the plant to "breathe," taking in carbon dioxide and giving off oxygen (the opposite of animals). Photosynthesis is the process by which the plant gets energy from the sun. Sunlight strikes chlorophyll and converts light energy into chemical energy. The plant uses the energy to convert carbon dioxide from the air into sugars that the plant needs for growth and development. Flowers contain the reproductive organs of the plant. Pollen from the male flower fertilizes the ovary of the female flower, which produces seeds, and then the cycle begins over again.

Keeping the same groups as before, have students research one of the following topics: land use in agriculture, water use in agriculture, and/or the water cycle. The search may be done online under the supervision of the teacher for younger students and/or at the school library. Each group will write up a short description and include simple diagrams, if appropriate, describing their topic. These will be handed in to the teacher for evaluation and assessment.

ACTIVITY FIVE
How Does Food Get From the Field to Your Plate?

A century ago, 75 per cent of Canadians lived on farms or in small towns and villages in the country. Farming then wasn't mechanized, so family and friends often pitched in to help the farmer bring in his crops.

Today, food is still produced by farmers. They plant and harvest crops, raise livestock for milk and meat and pick fruit and vegetables. Some farmers keep bees for making honey or tap maple trees for syrup. After being harvested, the food is picked up by truck and taken to the food processor.

Processing food means preparing the raw product and converting it into something where it can be preserved, stored, distributed, sold, and then consumed. For example, milk is refrigerated from the time it leaves the cow so it doesn't spoil. Fruits and vegetables have the leaves and stems removed, and are washed and stored, then packaged into bags and boxes for shipping to the store. Some fruits are crushed to make juice and others are cooked to make jam. Vegetables such as tomatoes are refrigerated so they remain fresh while corn and peas may be cooked then frozen so they can be sold in supermarkets later on.

Some other processing activities include: eggs being sorted by size and put into cartons; water being evaporated out of maple sap to make syrup which is then put into cans or glass containers; grain being milled into flour; and peanuts being crushed to make peanut butter. Virtually all food we buy is processed in some form or another.

After processing, the food is distributed to outlets across the country and even around the world. Now with super highways and refrigerated transport trucks, food can be distributed far and wide. This means that Canadians can also purchase food grown all over the world. Some farmers still sell their produce at roadside stands, mainly in the summer.

As householders, we don't grow as much food as we used to, so it means we need to go and buy it. Normally, that means going to the supermarket, to the bakery, or to a specialty store for fruits and vegetables. Food is also shipped directly to restaurants and fast food outlets, even the school cafeteria. Eating out is now a normal part of day-to-day eating.

ACTIVITY SIX
Drawing the Food to Table Story

Have students draw or illustrate the process that shows food being grown to the end point where it ends up in our refrigerators and/or on our tables. Students should choose one fruit or vegetable to depict in their drawings. The drawings can be done by hand, on a computer or a mobile device, or done as a storyboard if preferred. Use the following headings as a guideline:
- Getting Ready to Grow Food
- Growing the Food
- Moving the Food from the Field
- Processing the Food
- Selling the Food
- Storing the Food
- Preparing and Eating the Food

ACTIVITY SEVEN
The Farmer's Toolkit: Protecting the Food They Grow

Integrated Pest Management

What are the tools the farmer uses to safeguard crops, manage pests, and protect the environment? The farmer's toolkit consists of cultivation, crop rotation, fertilizers, good bugs, bug and weed resistant plants and chemicals.

Pesticides
Did you know that most food contains natural toxins? Some 99.9 per cent of toxins we ingest from products like raspberries, rhubarb, potatoes, and spinach are developed naturally to protect those crops from pests. Insects are a threat to cereal, oilseed, fruit and vegetable crops. Pesticides are used to control some 10,000 species that attack them. Over the years, new chemicals have been developed that are less harmful to people and animals. Many of these target specific pests and have very low use rates. They are more environmentally friendly. Pesticide use on crops has been reduced from litres or kilograms per hectare to millilitres or grams per hectare, and many pesticides biodegrade very quickly after use.

Note: Teachers should demonstrate in class, using containers, the difference between a litre or kilogram and a millilitre and gram.

Note: Did you know that North Americans spend about 11 per cent of their income on food? Without crop protection, it is estimated that food prices would rise by roughly 30 per cent. That means, the day-to-day food items we eat would become very expensive and some would be unaffordable. On a global level, without measures to protect food crops from insects, disease, and other threats, it is estimated that the current world fruit and vegetable production would drop from 50 per cent to 100 per cent depending on the location of the farm.

Fungicides
Plant disease comes from parasitic fungi where some 14,000 species affect crops around the world. The fungi affect crop yield and quality. For example, the infamous Irish Potato Famine in the 1840s, where some one million Irish starved to death and forced hundreds of thousands to leave their homeland, could have been avoided if a blight disease fungicide had been developed and the crop had been properly treated.

Herbicides
There are more than 2,000 types of weeds that take moisture, nutrients, and sunlight from crops, and that is why herbicides may be used to control their growth. Herbicides may be used on gardens, lawns, pasture, fields, and range lands. New products target specific weeds and biodegrade.

The Canadian government strictly regulates the use of all chemicals on crops. Each chemical is stringently tested and it takes a long time before it is licensed for use in the field. Chemical residue levels in crops are extremely low. Following are some examples illustrating how safe residue levels can be based on laboratory tests:

- A 68 kilogram (149 pound) adult could eat 3,000 heads of lettuce every day for a lifetime and not exceed a harmful level
- A baby could be fed 87 cups of applesauce each day
- An 18 kilogram (40 pound) child could eat 524 apples a day
- A four-year-old could munch 13,700 kilograms (30,203 lbs) of carrots every day
- A 60 kilogram (132 pound) adult could eat 180,000 kilosgrams (396,832 pounds) of bananas every day

Note: Teachers should bring into class a good apple (one that is blemish free and healthy-looking), and one that is in poor condition due to being attacked by bugs or a fungus or simply one that has started to spoil, for the purpose of demonstrating the difference between an apple that is protected in the field and one that may not be protected.

ACTIVITY EIGHT
An Apple A Day

Apples are the most important fruit tree crop in Canada; varieties include, McIntosh, Red Delicious, Empire, Spartan, and Cortland.

Note: Teachers should bring into class examples of different varieties of apples grown in Canada.

History of Apples in Canada

Fruit-growing was introduced to Nova Scotia by the early French settlers sometime in the early 1600s. They were a self-sufficient lot; each homestead had several apple trees. By drying apples, settlers could have the fruit available to them year-round to make pies, puddings, tarts, and many other dishes.

In 19th Century Quebec, seedlings were grown from seed imported from the U.S., France, England, and Russia. Fruit growing was a family affair; most family-owned orchards contained about 40 trees of varying varieties. In 1875, 25,000 bushels of apples were harvested in Quebec from about 21,000 apple trees. Most of this crop ended up in Montreal, and still today, most Quebec apples are destined for markets along the St. Lawrence River.

Historical records in Ontario indicate that apples were propagated in the Niagara region as early as 1790. By 1880, 84 apple varieties were in production in Ontario. Ontario's climate, geography and soils make it the perfect place to grow apples. The majority of the apple-producing areas in Ontario are spread along the shores of Lake Ontario, Lake Erie, Lake Huron and Georgian Bay. There are approximately 700 apple growers in Ontario. About half of Ontario's apples are sold fresh while the other half are used for processing into items such as apple juice, sauce, and pies.

Apples were introduced to Manitoba in 1874 using stock from Ontario and Russia. The harsh prairie climate discouraged growers, however in the 20th Century, breeders at University of Saskatchewan and the Canadian Department of Agriculture research farm at Morden, Manitoba, developed some hardy varieties.

Fruits from trees were introduced to British Columbia by the early settlers as seeds that they carried with them from Fort Vancouver, as they explored the interior of the province. By the 1850s, there were plantings of small orchards in the Fraser Valley. Growers, including an Oblate missionary named Father Pandosy, had discovered the Okanagan Valley, an area boasting a warmer, although much drier, climate. Pandosy planted his first trees where the City of Kelowna now stands. Dry soil proved a barrier to production until growers rigged pumps and open flumes to direct water from lakes and creeks into the Okanagan Valley.

Today, apple production is concentrated mainly in Ontario, British Columbia, and Quebec. In 2013 421,084 tonnes of apples were grown in Canada.

How Apples Grow

An apple farm is known as an orchard. Most apple farmers manage orchards that are approximately 20 acres in size—that is almost 20 football fields! While older orchards have tall apple trees spread out over the land, new orchards use "size-controlled" or semi-dwarf trees that are planted closer together—this allows farmers to grow more apples and care for the trees without having to use ladders.

There are more than 40 different pest species of insects and mites that can harm apples. While some bugs attack the fruit directly, others attack the tree—the bark, leaves, and roots—making it sick and unable to produce apples. Many fruit farmers take part in a program called "integrated pest management" that uses a variety of methods to help fight pest infestations. Beneficial insects and mites—good bugs—are used to eat the bugs that would normally destroy the apple tree and their fruit. New varieties of apple trees that are more resistant to bugs are also being created. Farmers often have to spray their trees with pesticides in order to kill the bugs. Farmers have also recently started to use "scouts" in their efforts to combat pests. These people monitor pest activity in orchards and are able to spot unwanted pests early and use one of these methods to remove them. It is through this balance of pest management methods that farmers are able to produce healthy crops and provide us with the apples we enjoy all year-round.

Examples of a few pests that can be found on apple trees:

Green Stink Bugs:
The green stink bug gets it name because of the foul-smelling liquid it releases when something disturbs it.

Apple Maggot:
The adult apple maggot is slightly smaller than a housefly, has a white dot on its thorax, and black banding on its wings looking like an 'F.'

Tarnished Plant Bug:
Adult tarnish plant bugs feed on apple buds by inserting their sucking mouth into the plant tissue.

Eastern Tent Caterpillars:
When eastern tent caterpillars hatch, they are small. They immediately climb up into the tree to juncture in the branches and build a silk tent.

Green Fruitworms:
The green fruitworm feeds on the leaves and fruit of apple trees.

White Apple Leafhopper:
An adult white apple leafhopper has sucking mouth parts, which it inserts into plant cells and removes the contents.

Eat Your Apples!

- Apples are a good source of fibre and Vitamin C
- When buying apples, choose firm ones that are free of wrinkles and bruises
- When storing, remove any apples that may be overripe—they give off gas that causes nearby apples to spoil
- Apples can be kept for up to one month in a plastic bag in the refrigerator
- Wash apples under cold water—using a brush if handy—and then buff before eating

ACTIVITY NINE
Going Buggy

Insects are everywhere! About 75 per cent of all animals known to man are insects. Just one area of forest soil (the size of two adult footprints), may contain more than 30,000 insects. Insects are essential to life on our planet, as they are a vital part of ecosystems. However, some bugs are more beneficial to the necessities of life than others.

Food producers in Canada have learned how to deal with harmful insects and also how to use beneficial insects to their advantage to ensure they can produce the appropriate amount of food to allow Canadians a wide variety of fresh food.

Five common bugs are:
Lady Beetle (ladybug)
Praying Mantis
Hornworm
Pepper Maggot
Stink Bug

Bug Information

Lady Beetle (Family: Coccinellidae)

- Known to everyone as ladybugs—even if they are male!
- Lady beetles are found worldwide, with over 4,500 different species
- Name comes from "Beetle of our Lady," recognizing their role in saving crops
- Two-spotted and seven-spotted varieties are often seen in Canada
- Aphids (small bugs that harm crops) are a lady beetle's favourite food
- The female beetle deposits their eggs in aphid colonies
- Almost as soon as they hatch, the beetles attack the aphids, helping get rid of pests

Praying Mantis (Family: Mantidae)

- The way they hold the front of their bodies makes them look like they are "praying"
- The name "mantis" comes from the Greek word for "prophet"
- The biggest varieties can grow up to 15 cm long
- They are carnivorous insects that almost always start eating the insect while it is still alive
- They are the only predator fast enough to catch mosquitoes and flies
- Praying Mantis are terrific pest exterminators; they help keep down the population of bugs that are a threat to farming

Hornworm (Family: Sphingidae)

- Gets its name from the prominent horn on its head
- Known for its distinctive seven or eight white lines down the side of its body
- As an adult, they transform into hawk moths
- Hornworms are a pest for farmers as they eat leaves right down to almost nothing
- In Canada, they feed on tobacco or tomatoes
- The larvae of the tobacco hornworm can become so chemically dependent on tobacco plants that they will starve to death rather than eat anything else

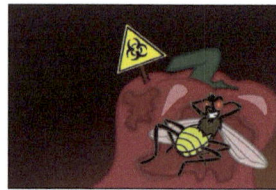
Pepper Maggot (Family: Tephritidae)

- The Pepper Maggot hurts eggplants and tomatoes in addition to peppers
- The female lays its eggs right inside the pepper (it prefers fleshy red peppers)
- The larvae feeds from inside the pepper as it grows, eventually breaking through the skin
- Damage from this insect can be devastating, as high as 90% of a crop
- The adult transforms into a brightly coloured yellow striped fly

Stink Bug (Family: Pentatomidae)

- Has a shield shaped body, often with very colourful markings
- The Stink Bug damages tomatoes, alfalfa, cereals, soybeans, beans, and peas
- They puncture the skin of the plant with their mouths and suck out plant juices
- Stink bugs can decimate crops and cause huge crop losses
- Oozes a foul smelling fluid from a pore on each side of their body to discourage predators

ACTIVITY TEN
The Bug Game

Things to do:

1. Create a Bug Game. Here's how it could work: Give each of the bugs a name and assign certain powers to them. They should also form a hierarchy, such as, one bug from each side is the most powerful and can trump all of the other bugs both good and bad. Have students create their own board game. The idea is either side has to capture the apple. In order to capture the apple, a journey must take place through various parts of a farm to the apple orchard. At each point in the journey, certain things can happen. For example, land on a certain spot and the farmer has sprayed a pesticide that sends the bad bug back several spaces and advances the good bug toward the apple. Land on another spot and the farmer has set traps for bad bugs that distract them, or good bugs are hindered by high winds during a windstorm. The idea is to create a series of simple obstacles using the farm as the centre of the action. Try to work in as many farm-related activities as possible and use the bug cards as the men that advance around the board. The board itself can be very simple. The class can be divided into groups at different times and each group can invent and design its own bug game. Remember, however, that the game should include as much factual information about what good and bad bugs do and how either may be hindered or advanced as they pursue their quest for the apple. Students should be as creative as possible and have fun with the games they create. Each group will then present its game to the rest of the class and have them spend part of a period trying out the other games that have been created.
2. Look the bugs up on the Internet or in the library to find out more information about them.
3. Have students draw their own pictures of these bugs or other bugs that protect and/or harm crops.
4. Have students pick a bug and storyboard what it does.
5. Have students write a story about one bug. Students can give the bug a name and create a character around it.

CULMINATING ACTIVITY
Head to the Hills

This activity applies all of the knowledge that has been acquired up to this point. The best way to apply it all in a practical way is to take a field trip to a local farm and talk to the farmer about what they do and how they ensure that their crops are both healthy and nutritious when they are delivered to the market.

Sample Questions:

1. How long does it take for the crops to grow?
2. How much time does the farmer spend in the field?
3. Besides planting, tending, and harvesting, what else does the farmer do?
4. How does the farmer ensure the crops are healthy and nutritious?
5. What sort of crop protection does the farmer use?
6. What would happen if the farmer did not protect the crops?
7. How many people can the farmer feed?
8. How has the technology for farming changed?
9. What effect does the weather have on the crops?
10. How many people work on the farm? What are their roles?
11. How does the farmer know the soil is good for planting? Does it ever wear out?
12. How does the farmer get water to the crops?
13. Does the farmer have any suggestions about how to feed a growing global population when the amount of land used to farm is shrinking?

Resources:

Agriculture in the Classroom: *www.aitc.ca*
Ontario Agri-Food Education: *www.oafe.org*
Statistics Canada – Agriculture at a Glance:
www.statcan.gc.ca/pub/96-325-x/96-325-x2014001-eng.htm

Lady Bug

Praying Mantis

Stink Bug

Horn Worm

Pepper Maggot

THE GOLD BOOK OF LESSON PLANS: VOLUME ONE

LESSON TWO

FUTURE WORLDS
STRUCTURING SOCIETY 50, 100, AND 200 YEARS INTO THE FUTURE

The astronauts in any potential mission to Mars will constitute the human building blocks for society in the future. It isn't inconceivable that space-based societies in the future may be populated by species other than humans. If scientific speculation is to be believed, out of the hundreds of millions of galaxies in the universe, it is possible other intelligent life forms might exist and then co-exist with their fellow species in some form of structured society.

GRADE LEVEL:
6 - 9

CURRICULA THEMES:

Social Studies
Language
History

CONVENTIONAL SOCIETAL MODELS ON EARTH

Monarchy

The most famous monarchy in existence today is the one that we most see and hear about in the media—the British monarchy. The royal traditions inherent in England and much of Europe have a rich and varied history. Monarchies are based on the rule of a royal house, as in the case of England where the House of Windsor currently sits on the throne. Royal rulers ascend through the divine right of kings (or queens) whereby the right to rule over a land such as England or France was originally determined by God. Although the current monarch in England (Queen Elizabeth II), is primarily a figurehead without real power, it was not always the case. Was the monarchy effective? What were its strengths and/or weaknesses? Why aren't there more monarchies today?

City-state

A city-state is a model that existed primarily in ancient Greek civilization, whereby a city such as Athens, Sparta, Thebes, Corinth, or Troy acted as if it were a country. Such societies enacted some of the democratic principles we see in existence today. For example, representatives might be elected to a governing body like a Senate, but the elections were only open to citizens of the city-state. There was a considerable slave population. Slaves were not eligible to vote. Elected representatives and rulers also tended to come from the aristocratic ranks rather than those of the commoners, with some exceptions. There were also great rivalries and ongoing wars between the city-states as they jockeyed for power in the known world. Is there a parallel between one of the ancient city-states and powerful cities in existence today, such as, New York, London, Paris, Moscow, Rio de Janeiro, Mexico City, New Delhi, Hong Kong, Seoul, the Greater Toronto Area (GTA), or Singapore?

Utopia

Utopia is based on the theories and writings first of the historical figure, lawyer, statesman, and writer, Sir Thomas More, and then popularized by philosopher, writer, and naturalist, Henry David Thoreau. This concept is based on a set of ideals, tends to be anti-materialistic, incorporates the idea of reason and rationality, and is often steeped in nature and "natural" premises. As such, utopia is more of a concept than a practical reality, although examples exist in the "back to the land" communal experiments of the 1960s and the contemporary Kibbutz in Israel. What are the benefits of this model? Why doesn't it exist in greater numbers?

Oligarchy

An oligarchy involves rule by a small group of powerful individuals (always men, it seems), who may be elected, appointed, or even inherit their positions of power in the society. It acts like a governing council and usually has an elected or appointed leader. Often the members come from the military, leading families, or those with important business interests. Conceptually, however, the oligarchy may be comprised of the few who are deemed worthy as determined by criteria set by societal norms and values.

Theoretically, members may be chosen on the basis of being the most honourable, the wisest, the most virtuous, and so on.

Democracy

Democracy is the model with which we are most familiar. It is the system under which we, in Western society, live but many countries around the world do not. It is important to note that democracy is an evolutionary system that emerged out of its predecessors. The system originated with the city-states that witnessed elections by the "people" or citizens of society for the purpose of governance. Within a democratic society, inherent rights are given to its citizens, who, in turn, elect members to represent their interests and points of view in a legislative body. As we know, there are a number of variations and interpretations of what constitutes democracy. There are significant differences between the way society operates in the United States, as compared to the United Kingdom, and compared to Canada, for example. In recent decades, a number of European countries have been "democratized," notably Poland, the Czech and Slovak Republics, the former East Germany, the Ukraine and even, Russia, where elections are now held to form governments.

Virtual Democracy

As technology has become more pervasive and networks proliferate, democracy has been given a new twist. The Internet and subsequent social networks that have sprung up are providing new democratic forums for anyone who is connected and has a point of view to share or a comment to make. Like-minded groups can band together online to support or promote a cause or issue. Individuals can have input into topics of interest and express an opinion, even criticize the status quo. In a sense, this is participatory democracy on a whole new level, no longer restricted by geography or time zone. Ideas, notions, trends, and fads proliferate in the virtual world. It is a force that has been harnessed for political purposes and has proven to be a powerful influence on attitudes and fashion. This virtual democratic milieu will evolve and form part of the society of the future in some shape or form.

Kleptocracy

This is a government that is often democratically elected, but something goes radically wrong in the process. That is, a group of influential officials band together to systematically loot the coffers of society, where corruption appears to be the modus operandi. Holding the levers of power means that the corrupt group of officials often controls the military and/or the police who provide the mechanisms to enforce a malevolent rule of law, as well as suppress any dissenting forces or groups. This model can apply to existing models such as an oligarchy or dictatorship. There are examples, however, where a democratically elected president or prime minister may have started out with good intentions, but could not resist the temptations before them after taking office. As a result, the society and the individuals within it suffer hardships including the loss of democratic and human rights.

Dictatorship

A dictatorship is essentially the rule of one individual who controls, through different means, all aspects of society. Society is then a reflection of that individual's personality, beliefs, and behaviour. If the dictator is deemed benevolent, then society may be as well. Otherwise, the society is a direct reflection of the dictator's personality and approach to governance. Modern-day examples may include, Joseph Stalin, Adolf Hitler, Benito Mussolini, and perhaps Chairman Mao. Earlier historical examples include, Napoleon Bonaparte, Alexander the Great, Genghis Khan, Hannibal, and Nero. If we look around the world today, we may see some modern examples of dictatorships. Why does this societal model exist? What is the historical context? Is it useful and if so, how? Some of the most fascinating historical and contemporary characters have been dictators, but we must decide if their role is one that can benefit society at all. You must decide if this is the model you wish to adapt when building your future world.

LEARNING OUTCOMES

Students will:
- Understand the structure and operation of society
- Gain insight into the relationship between past, present, and future
- Comprehend the complexity of human interrelationships
- Understand some technical aspects of communication systems
- Create, invent, and devise communications products and systems of the future
- Enhance socialization by working in teams
- Use critical thinking skills to solve problems and meet challenges

CURRICULUM CONNECTIONS

SOCIAL STUDIES

The Role of Technology in Social Studies, History, and Geography

Information and communications technology (ICT) provides a range of tools with a unique capacity to extend and enrich teachers' instructional strategies and students' learning in social studies, history, and geography. Information and communications technology can be used to connect students to other schools, at home and abroad, and to bring the global community into the local classroom. Computer programs can help students to collect, organize, and sort the data they gather and to write, edit, and present reports on their findings. The technology also makes it possible to use simulations—in geography, for instance—when field studies on a particular topic are not feasible.

Whenever appropriate, therefore, students should be encouraged to use ICT to support and communicate their learning. For example, students working individually or in groups can use mobile devices, computers, websites, and social media to gain access to museums and archives in Canada and around the world. Students can also use mobile devices and digital cameras and projectors to design, script, and present the results of their research to their classmates.

CANADA AND WORLD CONNECTIONS: Canada's Links to the World

GRADE 6

Overview

Students identify and describe Canada's economic, political, social, and physical links with the United States and other regions of the world. They use a variety of inquiry methods and research tools to investigate the importance of international connections for Canada's well-being and influence in the world. Students identify current international issues that concern Canada, and describe Canada's response to them.

Overall Expectations

Students will:
- Identify and describe Canada's economic, political, social, and physical links with the United States and other regions of the world
- Use a variety of resources and tools to gather, process, and communicate information about the domestic and international effects of Canada's links with the United States and other areas of the world
- Explain the relevance to Canada of current global issues and influences

LANGUAGE

GRADES 6–8

Oral Communication

Students will:
- Listen in order to understand and respond appropriately in a variety of situations for a variety of purposes
- Use speaking skills and strategies appropriately to communicate with different audiences for a variety of purposes
- Reflect on and identify their strengths as listeners and speakers, areas for improvement, and the strategies they found most helpful in oral communication situations

Reading

Students will:
- Read and demonstrate an understanding of a variety of literary, graphic, and informational texts, using a range of strategies to construct meaning
- Recognize a variety of text forms, text features, and stylistic elements and demonstrate understanding of how they help communicate meaning
- Use knowledge of words and cueing systems to read fluently
- Reflect on and identify their strengths as readers, areas for improvement, and the strategies they found most helpful before, during, and after reading

Writing

Students will:
- Generate, gather, and organize ideas and information to write for an intended purpose and audience
- Draft and revise their writing, using a variety of informational, literary, and graphic forms and stylistic elements appropriate for the purpose and audience
- Use editing, proofreading, and publishing skills and strategies, and knowledge of language conventions, to correct errors, refine expression, and present their work effectively
- Reflect on and identify their strengths as writers, areas for improvement, and the strategies they found most helpful at different stages in the writing process

Media Literacy

Students will:
- Demonstrate an understanding of a variety of media texts
- Identify some media forms and explain how the conventions and techniques associated with them are used to create meaning
- Create a variety of media texts for different purposes and audiences, using appropriate forms, conventions, and techniques
- Reflect on and identify their strengths, areas for improvement, and the strategies they found most helpful in understanding and creating media texts

HISTORY: MIGRATION
Grade 8

Students will:
- Identify factors that affect migration and mobility
- Demonstrate an understanding that migrations results from the decisions people make about conditions and events around them
- Identify factors that influence people to move away from a place (e.g., drought, war)

- Identify factors that influence people to move to another place (e.g., plenty of employment opportunities, security)
- Identify barriers to migration (e.g., physical, financial, legal, emotional)
- Use appropriate vocabulary (e.g., accessible, barriers, migration, mobility, immigration, emigration, refugees, modes of transportation, push factors, pull factors) to describe their inquiries and observations
- Locate relevant information from a variety of primary sources (e.g., surveys, statistics, interviews, field studies), and secondary sources (e.g., maps, illustrations, print materials, videos, websites)
- Communicate the results of inquiries for specific purposes and audiences, using media works, oral presentations, written notes and reports, drawings, tables, charts, and graphs
- Use a decision-making model to select an ideal place to live in or visit, and present this decision to other members of the class

ACTIVITY ONE

Students, working in teams will select a working model for a society of the future, one that may exist on Earth or a colony in space.

Background

History of Ancient Athens
www.sikyon.com/athens/athens_eg.html

History of Monarchy
www.en.wikipedia.org/wiki/Monarchy

History of Oligarchy
www.en.wikipedia.org/wiki/Oligarchy

History of the City-state
www.historyforkids.org/learn/government/polis.htm

Biography of Henry David Thoreau
www.biography.com/people/henry-david-thoreau-9506784#later-years&awesm=~oDBz4uRwynNnUL

Alvin Toffler, author of *Future Shock*
www.en.wikipedia.org/wiki/Alvin_Toffler
www.alvintoffler.net

Evolution of Democracy
www.en.wikipedia.org/wiki/Democracy

MATERIALS:

Computers, tablets, or mobile devices with Internet access
Writing or note-taking supplies or devices

DURATION:

One to three 45-minute periods

Evolution of Kleptocracy
www.en.wikipedia.org/wiki/Kleptocracy

History of Dictatorship
www.en.wikipedia.org/wiki/Dictatorship

Images of future worlds
www.google.ca/search?q=future+worlds&source=lnms&tbm=isch&sa=X&ei=Q0vZU-r7OpGeyAS8-oCgDA&ved=0CAYQ_AUoAQ&biw=1556&bih=982

Instructions

- Divide the class into teams of three or four students
- Students will research the societal models listed above, stating the pros and cons of each and whether any or all are relevant to a future world
- The research will be documented in a brief report, outlining each societal model and concluding with the one students select for their future world (Please note: It is acceptable to combine models if feasible or create one that is entirely new)
- The members of the team will discuss the societal model selected and how it might be developed to build a future world
- Student teams will identify the primary building blocks, values, and principles on which their future world is to be based
- Each member of the team will be assigned one area of the future world to develop and document, beginning with a description of its functionality, and major areas, including: government, citizenship, laws, banking/finance, communications/technology, and language/culture
- Each team member will present their findings to other members of the team

ACTIVITY TWO

Students working in teams will design a future societal model.

Background

Lesson plans on community building
www.lessonplanspage.com/SSLAOMDCommunityUnit-CommunityBuildingActivities36.htm
www.teach-nology.com/teachers/lesson_plans/history/comm

World Future Society-forecasts for the future
www.wfs.org/node/68

Design for the future
www.inhabitat.com
http://ubiquity.acm.org/article.cfm?id=345496

MATERIALS:

Computers, tablets, or mobile devices with Internet access, Large sheets of paper, markers, pencils, and pens

DURATION:

Four to Six 45-minute periods

Instructions

- Teams have already decided on their societal model in Activity One
- Have teams refer to their societal model and discuss how it might look as a chart or diagram
- Student teams will refer back to the resource links in Activity One and Activity Two above for background information
- Student teams will assign roles to each team member and devise a timeline for the drawing/designing of their future world with particular emphasis on how the components are connected and will function as a whole as well as where the team envisions this world existing, i.e., on Earth, or in space, or both
- Teams will include a write-up of approximately two pages describing their future world, its features and how it functions both as a structure, as well as serving the needs of its citizens
- Each student team will present their future world diagram to the rest of the class

ACTIVITY THREE

Students working in teams will demonstrate in a role-play how their future world responds to a crisis.

Background

Role-playing in the classroom
www.teachingenglish.org.uk/think/articles/role-play

Lesson plan that uses role-play to teach students about how Australia's government operates
www.peo.gov.au/teaching/mini-role-play-lesson-plans.html

Use of role-play in education
www.blatner.com/adam/pdntbk/rlplayedu.htm

Scenarios

1. A neighbouring world has threatened to declare war
2. Your future world is on the verge of running out of water
3. A group within your future world has declared a recent election null and void against the wishes of their opponents
4. All the power systems go down at the same time
5. The financial system has collapsed
6. The rulers of your future world decide there are too many people for society to support
7. The citizens of your future world go on strike
8. No one can take anyone else seriously in your future world

MATERIALS:

Computers, tablets, or mobile devices with Internet access, Large sheets of paper, markers, pencils, and pens

DURATION:

Two to Four 45-minute periods

Instructions

- Student teams will select a scenario listed above
- Each student team will create a five-minute role-play that explores the main issues of the dilemma they have chosen
- Each member of the team will be given a role to play, either behind the scenes (writing/directing), or as one of the actors in the role-play
- Student teams will script, then rehearse their role-play
- Each student team will present their role-play to the rest of the class
- Along with the presentation, a write-up of the role-play and the issues addressed must be handed in to the teacher for assessment

EVALUATION AND ASSESSMENT

General

Discussion

Level 1   Did not participate or contribute to the teacher-directed discussions
Level 2   Participated somewhat in the teacher-directed discussions
Level 3   Actively participated in the teacher-directed discussions
Level 4   Made a significant contribution to the teacher-directed discussions

Content

Level 1   Demonstrated limited understanding of concepts, facts, and terms
Level 2   Demonstrated some understanding of concepts, facts, and terms
Level 3   Demonstrated considerable understanding of concepts, facts, and terms
Level 4   Demonstrated thorough understanding of concepts, facts, and terms

Written Work

Level 1   Written report had many grammatical errors, is poorly structured and confusing
Level 2   Written report was generally clear, but has numerous grammatical errors
Level 3   Written report was well-structured and clear, but has a few significant/grammatical errors
Level 4   Written report was very clear, well-organized, with few errors

Oral Presentation

Level 1 Oral report was confusing, lacked emphasis and energy, with no discussion resulting
Level 2 Oral report was clear but lacked emphasis and energy, with little discussion resulting
Level 3 Oral report was clear and vibrantly presented, but lacked some emphasis and energy with a good discussion resulting
Level 4 Oral report was clear and enthusiastically presented, with energetic discussion resulting

Teamwork

Level 1 1 or 2 members dominated the team, very little co-operation
Level 2 Majority of the group made a contribution with some recognition of individual strengths, but co-operation was superficial
Level 3 Most members made a significant contribution, with a good level of co-operation
Level 4 All members made a significant contribution, individual strengths were recognized and used effectively, excellent co-operation among group members

Specific

Activity 1

Level 1 Student had little insight or understanding of the different societal models
Level 2 Student had basic insight or understanding of the different societal models
Level 3 Student had good insight or understanding of the different societal models
Level 4 Student had excellent insight or understanding of the different societal models

Activity 2

Level 1 Student made little effort and had little understanding of how to diagram the societal model selected
Level 2 Student made some effort and had some understanding of how to diagram the societal model selected
Level 3 Student made good effort and had good understanding of how to diagram the societal model selected
Level 4 Student made exemplary effort and had excellent understanding of how to diagram the societal model selected

Activity 3

Level 1   Student made little effort and had little interest in the development of the role-play

Level 2   Student made some effort and had some interest in the development of the role-play

Level 3   Student made good effort and had an active interest in the development of the role-play

Level 4   Student made an excellent effort and had an enthusiastic interest in the development of the role-play

LESSON THREE

INTERPLANETARY CITIZENSHIP

DECLARATION OF INTERPLANETARY RIGHTS AND RESPONSIBILITIES

The astronauts on the international space station or a future mission to Mars represent different nationalities, cultures, attitudes, outlooks, and genders. Once they blastoff for Mars, the astronauts form their own community. Within that community, there is a hierarchy of command, but the members know what constitutes their rights and responsibilities. And those rights and responsibilities, as applied to the mission, are different from those applicable to us who dwell on Earth. Within a community, however, even if it is in space, there are other rights and responsibilities that are remarkably similar to those experienced by anyone on the planet.

GRADE LEVEL:
6 – 9

CURRICULA THEMES:

Social Studies
Language

THE GOLD BOOK OF LESSON PLANS: VOLUME ONE

INTRODUCTION

Students will explore issues and themes around citizenship in space. The following activities will culminate in a Declaration of Interplanetary Citizenship. That is, each student will determine what that means or could mean to them in a personal sense and they will express that sentiment in some form of presentation to the rest of the class.

LEARNING OUTCOMES

Students will learn:
- To appreciate and safeguard the space/planetary environment
- To understand the differences between those of different backgrounds and cultures who work together in difficult circumstances, such as on the international space station, or a colony on Mars
- To understand and appreciate community values when living somewhere other than on the Earth
- To be accepting of others even if we don't agree with their point of view
- To deal with real 'universe' issues
- What rights and responsibilities come with interplanetary citizenship
- To understand what constitutes a moral choice when exercising the rights of interplanetary citizenship
- How to exercise interplanetary rights granted on Mars and elsewhere
- What the concept of an interplanetary community means
- What it feels like not to belong when living and working in space
- To see the connection between themselves and the interplanetary community
- To identify potential sources of conflict in space
- How to defuse situations when conflict arises in space
- To define interplanetary citizenship and create a declaration of the same
- To work together in teams
- To sharpen critical assessment skills

CURRICULUM CONNECTIONS

SOCIAL STUDIES

The Role of Technology in Social Studies, History, and Geography

Information and communications technology (ICT) provides a range of tools with a unique capacity to extend and enrich teachers' instructional strategies and students' learning in social studies, history, and geography. Information and communications technology can be used to connect students to other schools, at home and abroad, and to bring the global community into the local classroom. Computer programs can help students to collect, organize, and sort the data they gather and to write, edit, and present reports on their findings. The technology also makes it possible to use simulations—in geography, for instance—when field studies on a particular topic are not feasible.

Whenever appropriate, therefore, students should be encouraged to use ICT to support and communicate their learning. For example, students working individually or in groups can use mobile devices, websites, and social media to gain access to museums and archives in Canada and around the world. Students can also use mobile devices and digital cameras to design, script, and present the results of their research to their classmates.

CANADA AND WORLD CONNECTIONS: CANADA'S LINKS TO THE WORLD
GRADE 6-8

Overview

Students identify and describe Canada's economic, political, social, and physical links with the United States and other regions of the world. They use a variety of inquiry methods and research tools to investigate the importance of international connections for Canada's well-being and influence in the world. Students identify current international issues that concern Canada, and describe Canada's response to them.

Overall Expectations

By the end of Grade 6, students will:
- Identify and describe Canada's economic, political, social, and physical links with the United States and other regions of the world
- Use a variety of resources and tools to gather, process, and communicate information about the domestic and international effects of Canada's links with the United States and other areas of the world
- Explain the relevance to Canada of current global issues and influences

GRADE 6 LANGUAGE

Oral Communication

The Oral Communication strand has three overall expectations.

Students will:
- Listen in order to understand and respond appropriately in a variety of situations for a variety of purposes

- Use speaking skills and strategies appropriately to communicate with different audiences for a variety of purposes
- Reflect on and identify their strengths as listeners and speakers, areas for improvement, and the strategies they found most helpful in oral communication situations

Reading

The Reading strand has four overall expectations, as follows:

Students will:
- Read and demonstrate an understanding of a variety of literary, graphic, and informational texts, using a range of strategies to construct meaning
- Recognize a variety of text forms, text features, and stylistic elements and demonstrate understanding of how they help communicate meaning
- Use knowledge of words and cueing systems to read fluently
- Reflect on and identify their strengths as readers, areas for improvement, and the strategies they found most helpful before, during, and after reading

Writing

The Writing strand has four overall expectations, as follows:

Students will:
- Generate, gather, and organize ideas and information to write for an intended purpose and audience
- Draft and revise their writing, using a variety of informational, literary, and graphic forms and stylistic elements appropriate for the purpose and audience
- Use editing, proofreading, and publishing skills and strategies, and knowledge of language conventions, to correct errors, refine expression, and present their work effectively
- Reflect on and identify their strengths as writers, areas for improvement, and the strategies they found most helpful at different stages in the writing process

Media Literacy

The Media Literacy strand has four overall expectations, as follows;

Students will:
- Demonstrate an understanding of a variety of media texts
- Identify some media forms and explain how the conventions and techniques associated with them are used to create meaning
- Create a variety of media texts for different purposes and audiences, using appropriate forms, conventions, and techniques
- Reflect on and identify their strengths, areas for improvement, and the strategies they found most helpful in understanding and creating media texts

GRADE 8 HISTORY: MIGRATION

The Task

Each student chooses a country of origin, takes the role of a potential immigrant to Canada, and investigates the push and pull factors that might have an impact on his or her family's decision on whether to stay in that country, or to emigrate to Canada. Students develop summary statements that included their recommendations to their families and the supporting reasons for those recommendations.

Expectations

This gives students the opportunity to demonstrate their achievement of the following selected overall and specific expectations from the strand History: Migration.

Students will:
- Identify factors that affect migration and mobility
- Demonstrate an understanding that migrations results from the decisions people make about conditions and events around them
- Identify factors that influence people to move away from a place (e.g., drought, war)
- Identify factors that influence people to move to another place (e.g., plenty of employment opportunities, security)
- Identify barriers to migration (e.g., physical, financial, legal, emotional)
- Use appropriate vocabulary (e.g., accessible, barriers, migration, mobility, immigration, emigration, refugees, modes of transportation, push factors, pull factors), to describe their inquiries and observations
- Locate relevant information from a variety of primary sources (e.g., surveys, statistics, interviews, field studies), and secondary sources (e.g., maps, illustrations, print materials, videos, websites)
- Communicate the results of inquiries for specific purposes and audiences, using media works, oral presentations, written notes and reports, drawings, tables, charts, and graphs
- Use a decision-making model to select an ideal place to live in or visit, and present this decision to other members of the class

ACTIVITY ONE

MATERIALS:

Computers or mobile devices with Internet access, writing/note pads, pens, pencils, markers, construction paper, glue, safety scissors

DURATION:

Three to Five 45-minute periods

Students, working in teams will plan a community in space.

Background

www.un.org/en/documents/udhr (Universal Declaration of Human Rights)
www.davidsuzuki.org/about/declaration (Declaration of Interdependence)
www.nasa.gov/mission_pages/station/expeditions/expedition17/earth_day.html
  (Insight into the International Space Station—its own community in space)
www.nasa.gov/education/materials/#.U2pP5K1dXok (This site provides a link to NASA's resources for teachers.)
www.nasa.gov/audience/foreducators/teachingfromspace/dayinthelife/index.html
  (A day in the life at the International Space Station)
www.nasa.gov/audience/foreducators/edu-resources-for-shuttle-missions.html
  (This site provides educational resources about different space missions)
www.youtube.com/watch?v=ttYKVbz9bzo (Video introduction to the Marsville project)
www.freewebs.com/marsmen (A school-based Mars project)
http://schools.ednet.ns.ca/avrsb/732/obrien12/page7/files/MSIP-MarsActivities.pdf
  (Everything you need to know about Mars)
www.nasa.gov/mission_pages/station/main/index.html#.U2pRE61dXok (News on the International Space Station)
http://science.howstuffworks.com/living-in-space.htm (Article on living in space, check out the video on the space elevator)
www.spacefuture.com/habitat/living.shtml (Short article on living in space)
www.pbs.org/spacestation/station/living.htm (Insight into living in space)

Instructions

- Divide the class into teams of three or four students
- Have students review the two declarations above (The Universal Declaration of Human Rights and the Declaration of Interdependence)
- Within each group, students will have a discussion as to how these two declarations apply to humans living in space
- Student teams will write down 10 key points applying the declarations to colonizing space and each team will present their key points to the rest of the class
- The 10 key points form a framework for planning, then building, a community in space, i.e., first teams have to decide what sort of community they want in terms of social and cultural norms, then they must examine the technical and environmental aspects of creating such a community
- Each community will be given a name and an identity (flag, crest, logo, etc.)
- Referring to the links above and others found by searching online, student teams will record and plan out, the community they wish to build in space and will include mechanisms for accommodating citizens of different origin and means of dealing with challenges and conflict as they arise

- The teams will list the cultural, social and legal structure (e.g., an interplanetary constitution) they want in the community as well as providing a physical design for the environment, i.e., space pod, space station, biosphere and so on.
- Once the teams have sketched out their space-based communities, they will proceed to the second activity

ACTIVITY TWO

Students working in teams will design a community in space.

Background

www.lessonplanspage.com/SSLAOMDCommunityUnit-CommunityBuildingActivities36.htm (Lesson plans on community building)
www.teach-nology.com/teachers/lesson_plans/history/comm (More lesson plans on community building)
www.readwritethink.org/classroom-resources/lesson-plans/building-learning-community-crafting-991.html Community building in the classroom)
www.wfs.org/node/68 (World Future Society-forecasts for the future)

Instructions

- Teams have already created a community-building plan in Activity One
- Have teams refer to their plan and discuss how they can build a scale model of the community in space
- Student teams will refer back to the resource links in Activity One and Activity Two above for background information
- Student teams will select the tools they wish to use, i.e., construction materials or a digital design using computer and software
- Student teams will assign roles to each team member and devise a timeline for the creation of the community
- Along with the building/designing of the community, teams will include a write-up of approximately two pages describing their community in space, its features and how it functions both as a structure, as well as serving the needs of its citizens
- Each student team will present their model to the rest of the class

MATERIALS:

Computers or mobile devices with Internet access, design/layout software such as Adobe InDesign, Photoshop, Illustrator or other software, construction materials, plasticine, Lego, etc.

DURATION:

Four to Six 45-minute periods

ACTIVITY THREE

MATERIALS:

Any or all of the materials listed in Activities One and Two

DURATION:

One to Three 45-minute periods

Students working in teams or individually will devise their own Declaration of Interplanetary Citizenship.

Background

www.un.org/en/documents/udhr (Universal Declaration of Human Rights)
www.davidsuzuki.org/about/declaration (Declaration of Interdependence)

Instructions

- Students will reflect on what being part of a community means
- Students will write down the differences between living in a community on Earth and a community in space
- Students will write down any similarities between living in a community on Earth and a community in space
- Students will write a short story based on the life of a character living in a community in space, and within the story the character must confront an ethical dilemma or challenge
- Students will draw/illustrate/storyboard the story they have written
- Students will create their own personalized Declaration of Interplanetary Citizenship, i.e., what does being an interplanetary citizen mean to them personally?
- The Declaration of Interplanetary Citizenship may take any format students wish, i.e., song, poem, drawing, website, collage, mural, video, blog, vlog, etc.
- As time allows, the Declarations of Interplanetary Citizenship will be presented or put on display for the rest of the class to experience

EVALUATION AND ASSESSMENT

General

Discussion

Level 1   Did not participate or contribute to the teacher-directed discussions
Level 2   Participated somewhat in the teacher-directed discussions
Level 3   Actively participated in the teacher-directed discussions
Level 4   Made a significant contribution to the teacher-directed discussions

Content

Level 1   Demonstrated limited understanding of concepts, facts, and terms
Level 2   Demonstrated some understanding of concepts, facts, and terms

Level 3   Demonstrated considerable understanding of concepts, facts, and terms
Level 4   Demonstrated thorough understanding of concepts, facts, and terms

Written Work

Level 1   Written report had many grammatical errors, was poorly structured and confusing
Level 2   Written report was generally clear, but has numerous grammatical errors
Level 3   Written report was well-structured and clear, but has a few significant/grammatical errors
Level 4   Written report was very clear, well-organized, with few errors

Oral Presentation

Level 1   Oral report was confusing, lacked emphasis and energy, with no discussion resulting
Level 2   Oral report was clear, but lacked emphasis and energy, with little discussion resulting
Level 3   Oral report was clear and vibrantly presented, but lacked some emphasis and energy with a good discussion resulting
Level 4   Oral report was clear and enthusiastically presented, with energetic discussion resulting

Teamwork

Level 1   1 or 2 members dominated the team, very little co-operation
Level 2   Majority of the group made a contribution, with some recognition of individual strengths but co-operation was superficial
Level 3   Most members made a significant contribution, with a good level of co-operation
Level 4   All members made a significant contribution, individual strengths were recognized and used effectively, excellent co-operation among group members

Specific

Citizenship Issues

Level 1   Student had little insight or understanding of the relevance of rights and responsibilities of citizens
Level 2   Student had basic insight or understanding of the relevance of rights and responsibilities of citizens
Level 3   Student had good insight or understanding of the relevance of rights and responsibilities of citizens

Level 4   Student had excellent insight or understanding of the relevance of rights and responsibilities of citizens

Activity 1

Level 1   Student made little effort and had little understanding of community planning
Level 2   Student made basic effort and had some basic understanding of community planning
Level 3   Student made significant effort and had good understanding of community planning
Level 4   Student made excellent effort and had exemplary understanding of community planning

Activity 2

Level 1   Student made little effort and had little understanding of community designing
Level 2   Student made some effort and had some understanding of community designing
Level 3   Student made good effort and had good understanding of community designing
Level 4   Student made exemplary effort and had excellent understanding of community designing

Activity 3

Level 1   Student made little effort and had little interest in the development of a declaration of interplanetary citizenship
Level 2   Student made some effort and had some interest in the development of a declaration of interplanetary citizenship
Level 3   Student made good effort and had an active interest in the development of a declaration of interplanetary citizenship
Level 4   Student made an excellent effort and had an enthusiastic interest in the development of a declaration of interplanetary citizenship

LESSON FOUR

ROLL-A-COIN THROUGH THE CURRICULUM:
THE HISTORY OF CURRENCY

An exploration of significant people, places, and events through the evolution of Canadian currency. Students will also explore the value and importance of economic activity to the political and social existence in New France; how and why Canada became a country; the significance of amateur sport and its impact and importance for Canada; and how and why Canada was affected by its involvement in two world conflicts.

GRADE LEVEL:
Junior (4-6),
Intermediate (7-9),
Senior (10-12)

CURRICULA THEMES:

History, Social Studies, Language Arts, Geography

UNIT 1: NEW FRANCE

MATERIALS:

Pencils, markers, pens, paper, access to computers and the Internet

DURATION:

Two to Three 45-minute periods

Before Europeans ventured across the Atlantic Ocean, Canada was an unnamed, sparsely populated region inhabited by Aboriginal communities. It was a vast landscape waiting to be settled. The arrival of early French explorers and the founding of New France set off a chain of activities that led to the creation of Canada. The new country's unusual character was forged from an uneasy union between two European cultures that co-existed for centuries.

GENERAL OUTCOMES/EXPECTATIONS

Students will:
- Understand the conditions under which new settlers and new settlements existed
- Gain insight into the day-to-day existence of settlers
- See how the economy functioned and what part currency played in the local economy
- Conduct research using tools such as the Internet
- Hone critical assessment and evaluation skills
- Work together in teams to accomplish tasks

KEY CONCEPTS AND ISSUES

Students will explore the value and importance of economic activity to the political and social existence in New France.

JUNIOR LEVEL ACTIVITY
New France: Currency in the New World

Beginning with the founding of Quebec City in 1608, French settlements were established along the banks of the St. Lawrence River. Smaller communities, however, started earlier. Like any new enterprise, systems of government had to be set up from scratch. The lifeblood of any community is steeped in commerce and trade. And, although the barter system was in use for much of the trade that took place, hard currency was a neccessity. Merchants required payment for the goods they offered for sale. Members of the military who safeguarded early settlements, needed to pay their troops with some form of currency. For many of the early settlement years in New France, metal coins were a scarce commodity. These coins were transported from France. Once they were in circulation, a shortage developed. The settlements in New France were not capable or even allowed to produce their own currencies. Ships did sail back and forth to France, but did so infrequently. At times, the shortage of coins became so severe that an alternative was desperately needed. People who needed to be paid could not wait months, if not years, for ships to travel to France and back again. The solution was both creative and innovative. In the absence of metal coins, playing cards were introduced as currency. Although a novel solution, the practice became widely accepted within the new colonies. When troops were to be paid, for example, senior officers would write the denomination on the back of the playing card, displaying its value. To the merchants and the general population in the settlements, the playing cards became accepted currency.

OUTCOMES/EXPECTATIONS

Students will:
- Gain insight into the history of New France
- Understand what it was like to live during that period
- Research New France's monetary system
- Create an effective presentation
- Develop critical thinking and analytical skills
- Work together in teams

RESOURCES

www.historicacanada.ca
www.thecanadianencyclopedia.com
www.cbc.ca
www.collectionscanada.gc.ca

ACTIVITES

Working in teams of two to four, students will:

Research
Investigate the history of coins in Canada using the Internet.

Discuss
Within the teams, discuss what has been discovered about the history of coins in Canada.

Write
Each team will write a brief summary of their research findings: half-page in length.

Design
Each team will design a set of playing cards as currency representing coin denominations that could be used in New France. These cards could be used to purchase goods and services in the settlements.

Present
Each team will present the card designs to the class, explain what the designs represent, and illustrate how the cards would be used in a settlement.

Extension Activity

The student teams will design a new set of coins for use in New France. Based on their currency and on how much money it would take to buy something like a pound of flour or grain, the teams will come up with price lists for a range of goods that might be offered for sale in a settlement. By going through this exercise, students will gain insight into the economic life of the settlers. The teams will present their coin designs and price lists to the rest of the class.

INTERMEDIATE LEVEL ACTIVITY
New France: Community Life in New France

MATERIALS:

Pencils, markers, pens, paper, access to computers and the Internet

DURATION:

Two to Three 45-minute periods

The early European settlements began on the banks of the St. Lawrence River. Soldiers and sailors, sent over by the king of France, were the first people to reach the shores of this new land. It was already known that this new territory was rich in resources such as timber, fish, and beaver, whose pelts became extremely popular in Europe. While gold and diamonds were yet to be discovered, they were, however, on the minds of both those voyaging across the ocean and those who had sent them on the trip. Knowledge of these commodities came from the earliest European explorers, people such as John Cabot, Jacques Cartier, and Samuel de Champlain. (For more information visit: *www.historymuseum.ca/virtual-museum-of-new-france/the-explorers*) In fact, the early European explorers were sent for the specific purpose of seeking out whatever riches could be found and sent back to the respective king or queen, and to claim territory for the crown. Nobody thought about the people who, for thousands of years, had inhabited and owned the lands we now call Canada.

OUTCOMES/EXPECTATIONS

Students will:
- Gain insight into the day-to-day life of inhabitants in New France through research
- Understand the way in which the local economy worked
- Assume the role of a merchant advertising wares for sale
- Create an advertising flyer, newspaper advertisment or town crier announcement
- Work cooperatively in teams
- Present their findings orally and discuss the strategy and approach of the kind of advertising each team has created
- Develop critical thinking and analytical skills

RESOURCES

www.historicacanada.com
www.thecanadianencyclopedia.com
www.cbc.ca
www.collectionscanada.gc.ca

ACTIVITIES

Working in teams of two to four, students will:

Research
Investigate the lives and adventures of early explorers. Each team will select two explorers from the list below:
- Cartier, 1534-1536
- Champlain, 1604-1616
- Brûlé, 1615-1621
- Nicollet, 1634
- De Quen, 1647
- Des Groseilliers, 1654-1660
- Radisson, 1659-1660
- Perrot, 1665-1689
- Cavelier de La Salle, 1670-1687
- Albanel, 1672
- Marquette, 1673-1675
- Jolliet, 1673-1694
- Greysolon Dulhut, 1678-1679
- Hennepin, 1678-1680
- Lahontan, 1684-1688
- Chevalier de Troyes, 1686
- Le Moyne d'Iberville, 1686-1702
- Lamothe Cadillac, 1694-1701
- La Vérendrye, 1732-1739

Purpose
The purpose of this research is to gain insight into how New France became established and how the Europeans interacted with the Aboriginal peoples they encountered. In addition, students will gain insight into how community life began and existed. Each team will prepare a half-page report on each of the explorers selected. This research will help set the background for understanding the lives of those who inhabited the settlements. Each team will highlight any commercial transactions they come across while researching their selected explorers, including interactions explorers may have had with the native population and with those in their own community. For example, did the explorers trade commodities for beaver pelts and other furs? If so, what did they trade? Document the early forms of commerce that may have occurred.

Next step
Now, leap forward to project life in an early settlement such as Hochelaga and Stadacona. Search the Internet using a search engine to acquire background information and document, in point form, any information that the team finds on settlement life. In particular, the team should look for information about goods

and supplies that settlers required to sustain their lives, and what forms of economic activity occurred. Share this information among team members.

Create

The teams will draw on the research information to create an advertising campaign that maintains the tone and character of the period (1720s, for example). They must select a merchant (male, female, or establishment) and determine what sort of goods or services this merchant has for sale. The team must decide how they will promote this business to the inhabitants of the settlement by means of a flyer, a newspaper, a town crier, use of a troupe of actors, or something else. The first step after determining what goods are to be sold and at what price, will be to storyboard the advertising campaign. The storyboard may be drawn by hand or with the use of a computer. For information about storyboards, please see the following websites or use an Internet search engine.

http://accad.osu.edu/womenandtech/Storyboard%20Resource

Present

Each team will present its advertising campaign to the class and will discuss the campaign strategy and the pricing of its advertised goods.

Extension Activity

The student teams from the previous activity have created an advertising campaign promoting wares for sale dating from the 1700s in New France. As a group, the class will create its own settlement market, offering its wares for sale. The wares don't have to be real, but may be represented by a coupon or scrip. The challenge, however, will be for teams to purchase goods needed for the following scenarios:
- A two-week canoe trip down the St. Lawrence River, for at least two, but not more than four people
- A new household in the settlement supporting a mother, father, and two young children (the teams may assume that the family has brought certain items with them from their former home in France)
- A baker who is setting up shop in the settlement
- A shoemaker who is servicing the needs of the settlement
- Something/someone selected by the team

SENIOR LEVEL ACTIVITY
New France: Bringing New France to Life

The early European settlements were founded on the banks of the St. Lawrence River. Soldiers and sailors, sent over by the king of France, were the first people to reach the shores of this new land. It was already known that this new territory was rich in resources such as timber, fish, and beaver, whose pelts became extremely popular in Europe. While gold and diamonds were yet to be discovered, they were, however, on the minds of both those voyaging across the ocean and those who had sent them on the trip. Knowledge of these commodities came from the earliest European explorers, people such as John Cabot, Jacques Cartier, and Samuel de Champlain. In fact, the early European explorers were sent for the specific purpose of seeking out whatever riches could be found and sent back to the respective king or queen, and to claim territory for the crown. Nobody thought about the people who, for thousands of years, had inhabited and owned the lands we now call Canada.

MATERIALS:

Pencils, markers, pens, paper, access to computers and the Internet

DURATION:

Four to Six 45-minute periods

OUTCOMES/EXPECTATIONS

Students will:
- Develop a role-play where the characters are based on inhabitants of settlements in New France
- Produce a detailed script for the role-play that is to be created
- Conduct research using the Internet to find relevant information
- Work in teams to research, develop, and create the role-play
- Perform the role-plays for the rest of the class
- Hone critical thinking and analytical skills
- Use media that is appropriate for the specific projects

RESOURCES

www.canadianheritage.org/books/canada3.htm
www.archivescanadafrance.org (click on links)

ACTIVITIES

Working in teams of two to four, students will:

Divide
Students will be divided into teams of four or five and engage in a role-playing activity that will require their collective skills and efforts, as they work together to create the role-play.

Research
Student teams can either refer to the websites listed above, or alternatively, search the Internet using the phrase "life in New France."

Summarize
Each team will summarize its findings in point form. Maximum length: one page. For research and background information, teachers may also refer to the information detailed in the Intermediate Level Activity.

Points to consider
Using the resources listed, teams will examine the roles of men, women, and children as well as look at the differences between rural and urban life. In the early days of the settlements, the area and size of these early towns and villages were limited, which meant that many new settlers lived on farms and pursued the agricultural way of life. The social and legal doctrines were not as stringent in the farming communities, yet families fell into a distinct pattern of behaviour. Factor in the influence of the clergy, the military, and interactions with Aboriginal communities.

Discuss
Each team will discuss their research, and decide what roles to feature in their role-play (farmer, farmer's wife, soldier, child, merchant and/or priest), and determine the responsibilities.

Format
The role-play may take a number of different formats. It is up to each team to determine how to proceed. For example, it may take the form of a short scripted play or encounter, where the players pretend to live in New France and respond or interact as they imagine they would have in the days of New France. The format may follow that of an interview in which the characters are asked questions about their lives in New France.

Script
The role-play must be scripted or storyboarded in whatever format the team selects. (For background information on storyboarding, please see links above in the unit on the Intermediate Level Activity).

Present
Each team will perform their role-play for the class. After each has been presented, the class will give feedback on what it learned.

Extension Activity
As part of the role-play, the presentations may be audio or video taped. Role-plays may be presented within a talk show format, where a host conducts the interviews, and the guests represent a figure from New France. Technical assistance will be needed to record the presentation.

This activity will also require a post-production phase, in which the tape is edited for video and/or sound. Music may also be woven into the production.

UNIT 2: CONFEDERATION

SCENARIO

It took 132 years to complete Confederation. Completion came with the creation of the newest territory, Nunavut, in 1999. Prior to that, Newfoundland was the last province to join Confederation, in 1949. Not all provinces were created in 1867 when the British North America Act was written. Most came into being after that date and joined Confederation later.

Provinces and territories and the year they joined Confederation

Alberta—1905
British Columbia—1871
Manitoba—1870
New Brunswick—1867
Newfoundland—1949
Northwest Territories—1870
Nova Scotia—1867
Nunavut—1999
Ontario—1867
Prince Edward Island—1873
Quebec—1867
Saskatchewan—1905
Yukon Territory—1898

Influential people in Confederation by province/territory

Alberta—Frederick William Alpin Gordon Haultain
British Columbia—Amor De Cosmos
Manitoba—Louis Riel
New Brunswick—Samuel Leonard Tilley
Newfoundland—Joseph Roberts Smallwood
Northwest Territories—David Laird
Nova Scotia—Joseph Howe, Charles Tupper
Nunavut—Paul Okalik
Ontario—John Alexander Macdonald
Prince Edward Island—James Colledge Pope
Quebec—George-Étienne Cartier
Saskatchewan—Frederick William Alpin Gordon Haultain
Yukon—Samuel Benfield Steele

Problems
As a result of a number of difficulties they continued to face, the four original provinces considering Confederation saw distinct advantages in uniting.

Politics
Ontario and Quebec were initially known as the Province of Canada. The split came later. The provincial government didn't operate smoothly because the English in Ontario and the French in Quebec did not agree on how to make things work. Politicians thought that by joining together with the other colonies, these problems could
be solved.

Economics
Markets within the colonies were limited. Joining together would allow the colonies to market and sell goods to each other.

Military
The United States fought and won a war of independence against Great Britain. Great Britain also supported the South against the North during the American Civil War. After the Civil War ended, many Americans were angry with Britain and wanted to invade the territory that is now part of Canada. Great Britain believed that if Canada became an independent country, there would be less chance of an American invasion.

Railroads
The colonies had invested in building railway lines but had run into money troubles. It was clear to the politicians that a national railway running coast-to-coast was a top priority. Individually, however, the colonies could not afford it. The provincial politicians believed that a united Canada could finance the national railroad initiative.

Conferences
Leaders from the colonies organized a series of conferences at which the idea of Confederation was discussed.

Charlottetown Conference, September 1864
Politicians from the Province of Canada, New Brunswick, Nova Scotia, and Prince Edward Island met to discuss the idea of a political union.

Quebec Conference, October 1864
The leaders met once again to work out more of the details of running a country. Although the leaders from Newfoundland and Prince Edward Island participated in the discussions, they elected not to join Confederation at that time.

London Conference – December 1866-January 1867
The leaders from New Brunswick, Nova Scotia, and the Province of Canada met in London, England to formulate a final draft of their resolutions from the Quebec Conference. The final document, approved by the British Parliament, became known as the British North America Act. Canada was now a country.

July 1, 1867
Canada officially became a country with four original provinces. Two of these provinces—Ontario and Quebec—were formed when the Province of Canada split into two. It would take a long time before all provinces and territories joined the nation. Canada became a country, but a reluctant one.

GENERAL OUTCOMES/EXPECTATIONS

Students will:
- Understand how Canada became a nation and what conditions led to this event
- Gain insight into the key individuals who played a role in Canada becoming its own nation
- See how the country evolved geographically as other provinces and territories joined Confederation
- Research the building of the Canadian Pacific Railroad and determine its significance and impact on the country
- Understand how the fundamentals of the economy worked in a brand new nation
- Hone critical assessment and evaluation skills
- Work cooperatively in teams
- Relate historical and contemporary events to determine how one may have influenced the other

KEY CONCEPTS AND ISSUES

Students will explore how and why Canada became a country, who was involved, and the economic factors that led to Confederation.

JUNIOR LEVEL ACTIVITY
Confederation: Creating the Currency

MATERIALS:

Paper, pens, markers, computers with Internet access, drawing software (optional), media tools like PowerPoint (optional)

DURATION:

Two to Three 45-minute periods

OUTCOMES/EXPECTATIONS

Students will:
- Research the history of the banking system in Canada
- Understand the importance of the banking system to the economic well-being of the country
- Design a set of original coins to be used as currency
- Use appropriate visual tools in the creation of the coin sets
- Work together cooperatively in teams
- Hone critical thinking and analytical skills
- Support the coin designs with text that sustain their recommendations

RESOURCES

www.currencymuseum.ca/national-currency-collection
www.wikipedia.org/wiki/History_of_canadian_currency

INTRODUCTION

Discuss
Have a general discussion in class about money and its role in society. Why do we have it? What is it used for? What would happen if we didn't have money? How would people buy things if there wasn't any money? Are there alternatives to money? If so, what are they? List some of the key discussion points on the board.

Introduce
Specifically, introduce the topic of currency. How important are coins? Do they have a practical value? Tell the class, it will work in teams to design original sets of coins. As part of the work involved in designing these new coins, teams must research the use and history of coins in Canada. Inform the class that the designs it selects for their coins should be symbolic of an important idea or theme. For example, the sets of coins may have themes relating to nature, the environment, Canadian history, and so on.

Divide
Divide the class into teams of three or four students.

Research
Referring to the websites listed above, have student teams research the history of coins in Canada. They should discover how coin making evolved in the country and how coins are produced today by the Royal Canadian Mint.

Assign

Within each group, decisions must be made about who will do what. The group needs to figure out what coins they will design, the denominations, and the kinds of tools required to complete the designs: markers, paper or, if desired, more sophisticated design programs. It is up to the group to decide. Text explaining the importance of the design and what it represents must accompany each coin design.

Present

Each team will present their coin designs to the rest of the class, and explain the significance of the designs and what they represent.

EXTENSION ACTIVITY

If the student teams have access to PowerPoint and are familiar with this presentation software, they may adapt their class coin presentation using this technology. This will allow students to integrate the use of images, text, audio and even video, if applicable, to create a more professional presentation, while taking advantage of media tools. Students should storyboard their presentation before entering it into PowerPoint. Now that students have created their currencies, why not put them to work? What good is money unless it is spent? As a class, set up a market or bazaar where the currencies in use are those created by the teams. Team members will work together to set themselves up as their merchant of choice. They will select what wares they wish to sell. Those who come to their "stall" must negotiate the price of a particular item. Team members must decide prices ahead of time. If it happens that a buyer and seller have different currencies, they must negotiate the relative value and figure out the rate of exchange. (For example, two shekels may equal three zlotys and so on.) Have team members take turns as buyers and sellers of the wares. Please note: the –"wares"– do not have to be real items. They can be virtual items or articles depicted in a drawing or model made from clay, modelling clay, popsicle sticks, pipe cleaners, and so on.

INTERMEDIATE LEVEL ACTIVITY
Confederation: Connecting the Country

MATERIALS:

Paper, pens, pencils, markers, various art supplies, Computers with Internet access, drawing software optional

DURATION:

Four to Six 45-minute periods

OUTCOMES/EXPECTATIONS

Students will:
- Research the history of the railroad in Canada
- Understand the importance of the railroad to Canada's sovereignty and economic well-being
- Investigate why the government of Sir John A. Macdonald was defeated
- Write a series of articles analyzing the Canadian Pacific Railway bribery scandal
- Design a commemorative medallion that represents the completion of the railroad
- Present their projects to the class
- Hone critical thinking and analytical skills
- Work cooperatively in groups
- Use appropriate media tools

RESOURCES

www.cprheritage.com/history.htm
www.railways.incanada.net/candate/candate.htm
www.cprheritage.com/index.htm

INTRODUCTION

Have students review the information above in the introductory section of Confederation. At the time of Confederation, regional railroads existed. While recognizing the importance of a national railroad, the provinces could not afford to build a railroad from coast-to-coast. This was another reason that the original four provinces united in Confederation. The railroad helped convince the Western provinces, that they too, should join Confederation. They joined some years after 1867. Alberta and Saskatchewan, for instance, joined the Dominion of Canada in 1905. This was 28 years after the original four provinces formed the basis for the country. To mark Alberta's and Saskatchewan's centenary in 2005, the Royal Canadian Mint produced special commemorative coins. The government of Saskatchewan gave away 30,000 of their centennial coins to students.

Introduce

Introduce the topic of isolation versus unity into a classroom discussion. Have students imagine a vast territory where each region, territory or province was self-contained because there was no physical connection between them. Are there advantages to a region being isolated? If so, what might they be? What advantages, if any, are there in having a relatively rapid mode of transport between long distances? What are the economic advantages? What are the political advantages? Make a list on the board based on student suggestions.

Form
Form the class into teams of three or four students each. Using the resources listed above, have each team research the history of Canada's national railroad.

Storyboard
Each group will develop a chronological timeline depicting the development of Canada's national railroad from 1836 to the last spike driven into the Canadian Pacific Railway (CPR) in 1885. Along with a simple text narrative, each group will storyboard their timeline. Please see Resources in Community Life in New France for storyboarding techniques.

Write
Each group member will write a story about the completion of the CPR. Students will write from the perspective of journalists covering the event of the last spike. Remember to include background information about the railway scandal and why it brought down Sir John A. Macdonald's government. Some group members may prefer illustrating the story to writing it. Remember to include some text about the importance of this story and what it meant to the country. Why should anyone care about the completion of this railway line? Stories will be given to the teacher for evaluation.

Design
Each team will work together to design and, if possible, produce a commemorative medallion depicting an interpretation of the last spike and what it symbolizes or represents to Canada. Include a short narrative description of the medallion, explaining its meaning, significance, and the reasons for the design.

Present
Each team will present its medallions to the rest of the class. Students will discuss the designs, how they came up with the ideas and concepts, and what the medallions represent. Each presentation should last no more than five minutes.

EXTENSION ACTIVITY

Each team may be given the opportunity to adapt one aspect of the previous activities to a PowerPoint presentation. The team may opt for stories written about the last spike, adapt the storyboard for the railway timeline, or build a presentation around the commemorative medallion. Each team will show their PowerPoint presentation to the class.

SENIOR LEVEL ACTIVITY
Confederation: Politics and other Things

MATERIALS:

Pens, paper, computers with Internet access

DURATION:

Six to Ten 45-minute periods

OUTCOMES / EXPECTATIONS

Students will:
- Research the history of Confederation
- Gain a sense of the major political players in each province and territory
- Be exposed to both the positive and negative aspects of politics
- Understand how to deal with adversity through the examples of historical figures
- Get a sense of how their own province/territory responded to the invitation to join the Dominion of Canada
- Bring historical personalities to life through the creation of a one-act play
- Work cooperatively in teams
- Hone critical thinking and analytical skills

RESOURCES

www.historicacanada.ca (search Confederation)
www.cbc.ca (search Confederation)

INTRODUCTION

Discuss
First, set the context for the class. Refer to the background information in the main introduction that lays out the groundwork leading up to Confederation, the political players involved in forming Canada, and the conditions and events leading up to Confederation. Next, have a general discussion around the topic of Confederation. Determine how students think and feel about it. What, if anything, does Confederation mean to them? Why is it or is it not important? How would the formation of Canada as a country compare to that of the United States for example? Draw examples from current events. For instance, new countries and political systems are forming in places like Iraq, the Ukraine, and Afghanistan. How important is the ability to have a participatory democracy to the people in these countries? Do we, in Canada, take our democracy for granted?

Select
Have students select one of the provinces and territories.

Research
Each student will research their history of the selected province or territory and the circumstances leading up to its joining Confederation.

Write
Students will each write a summary of their research findings. Maximum length: two pages.

Select
From the list of people on page 59, each student will select one of the personalities who influenced the move to Confederation.

Research
Each student will research the personality selected.

Write
Each student will write a summary of the research they've compiled on the person they selected. Maximum length: one page.

Form
The teacher will divide the class into groups of three or four. Groups will be asked to create a one-act play based on the research they've undertaken so far.

Share
Each member of the group will share the information they've compiled on the provinces/territories and people.

Discuss
Group members will discuss ideas for a one-act play based on their shared information.

Research
The group will research one-act plays using the resources below and any other resources they wish:
www.lazybeescripts.co.uk/OneActPlays/Index.htm
www.playwriting101.com/chapter01

Assign
Team members will decide who does what. For instance, who will write the one-act play? Will it be a collaborative effort? Who will act in it? The play should be no more than five to seven minutes in length and should illuminate an aspect of Confederation based on the previous research.

Write/Rehearse
Team members will write and then rehearse their one-act play. A minimum of five rehearsals is required.

Perform
Each team will perform its one-act play for the class.

EXTENSION ACTIVITY

The Currency Summit

From information presented earlier, we know that for many years, Canada and its preceding provincial entities struggled to be consistent with the coins that circulated. Many different types of coins and systems of currencies were used. This made trading confusing and unreliable. The ongoing scarcity of coins also affected the economy. Local economies improved and stabilized once a solution was found. The solution addressed what currency was to be used in day-to-day transactions by buyers and sellers.

We also know that Canada came together as a country for practical reasons: to strengthen the economies of each of the founding provinces; to complete a national railway; and to strengthen defence when viewing the potential for invasion and other military incursions. The men who met to discuss the creation of a country were practical and knew that forming a country made sense for many reasons. Confederation then, the making of Canada, may be viewed in one context as a large, commercial transaction—a business deal.

Scenario

The four founding provinces have just come together as the new country known as Canada. Students now become members of the newly-formed Ministry of Finance, as created by one of the first acts of Parliament. The first significant task given to this new ministry is to convene a Currency Summit and develop a Canadian currency. Divide the class into teams and assign each team or a group of teams, projects to complete. Teams will report to the Summit on their research. Project teams will be given their tasks from the following list of assignments:

- A team will be required to determine what metals to use in the production of coins. They should research which metals are best, determine which metals to use, identify the source of the metals, and decide how the new mint will collect these metals. How can the ministry assure the Mint that there will be no shortage of appropriate metals? The project team will make a presentation on the above to the Summit.
- Once the metal supply has been determined, the next project team will need to determine and outline in detail how the coins will be made. What are the processes involved? The project team will create a PowerPoint presentation to report on the results. They will make recommendations on resources required, processes, methodologies and technologies to be employed.
- Given that the metal supply has been established and the minting process studied, the next project team will need to determine how the newly-minted coins will be circulated. They must also determine the relative value of these coins so consumers can decide what they can buy with their new coins. A system of denomination must be established and it must correspond to goods for sale in the marketplace. The team will report their findings to the Summit.
- Slowly, the infrastructure for the new coin system is being established, at least in

theory. The next project team will determine how consumers, everyday people in the community, will find out about the new coins as they are issued. Will they hear a town crier in the marketplace? Will a proclamation or discreet communication be issued? The team must determine how many coins to produce and how to circulate these coins. In other words, they need to develop a distribution system.
- The new government of Canada wishes to replace all of the old coins with new ones. That means, it must convince people to give up their old coins. This last project team will create a plan to communicate to people that the new coins are superior and should be used while the former coins will be discontinued and redeemed by the government. The project team must develop a way to promote the new coins and reacquire all of the old ones.

The team will present its plan to the Summit.

UNIT 3: THE WAR YEARS

The war years refers to the periods of 1914-1918 and 1939-1945. During the First World War, Canada became involved as part of the British Empire and managed to prove itself in a bloody conflict. In particular, the Canadians took the lead and prevailed in the Battle of Vimy Ridge which, in many ways, marked a turning point in the country's evolution on the global stage. The Canadians accomplished something their allies could not. In 1939, Canada declared war on another country for the first and only time in its history. Like the First World War, this second global conflict changed Canada and its people dramatically and irrevocably. War presents new and difficult challenges for nations, and Canada was no exception. In the Second World War, Canadians were called upon to learn new skills, to develop new strategies, and to rely on themselves, and each other, more than ever before. Where the First World War marked Canada's debut on the world stage, the Second World War accelerated the country's industrial capacity, its spirit and independence… all at a heavy price.

GENERAL OUTCOMES/EXPECTATIONS

Students will:
- Understand the impact of global war domestically and internationally
- Research the conditions and events that led to the first two world wars
- Gain insight into the economics of war
- Attempt to understand war through culture, specifically, visual arts and poetry
- Explore key issues such as conscription and what effect it had on the psyche of the country
- Work together cooperatively in teams
- Hone critical assessment and evaluation skills

KEY CONCEPTS AND ISSUES

Students will explore how and why Canada was affected by its involvement in two world conflicts, and what influence these events had on the evolution of the country.

JUNIOR LEVEL ACTIVITY
The War Years: Painting the Conflict

MATERIALS:

Art supplies, pens, paper, markers, pencils, computers with Internet access

DURATION:

Three to Four 45-minute periods

Lord Beaverbrook (Max Aitken) officially started Canada's war art program in 1916. Artists from Canada and around the world were commissioned to document the ongoing European conflict we know as the First World War. As a result, some 800 works of art were produced depicting civilians and the military, the battlefronts, and conditions at home. Often created under dangerous and difficult conditions, these works of art represent a valuable and all-too-human archive of the conditions surrounding warfare. The artists brought their own creativity and interpretation to the images they saw before them. As a result, an invaluable and poignant legacy was created and is available to those of us who have not experienced war first-hand. None of the commissioned works were exhibited during the First World War. These works were displayed publicly after the war's end. Canada was the first country to establish a war art program.

OUTCOMES/EXPECTATIONS

Students will:
- Research the history of Canadian art and war
- Research the artists who were sent overseas to document the war years
- Understand the role art plays in documenting wars
- Create a poster or visual display on a war-related theme or event
- Use critical thinking and analytical skills
- Apply knowledge to current events
- Work cooperatively in teams

RESOURCES

www.thecanadianencyclopedia.ca/en/article/war-artists
www.warmuseum.ca/cwm/exhibitions/canvas/1/cwd2e.shtml
www.veterans.gc.ca/eng/remembrance/history/artwork

ACTIVITIES

Discuss
Have a general discussion about art and its role as a vehicle for documenting events. Since war artists played an important role during earlier historical conflicts such as the American Civil War, their role was already well established.

Research
Students will research the history of Canadian war art.

Write
Students will summarize their research findings. Maximum length: one page.

Select
Students will select a war artist from the list above (see Resources). Students will summarize the life and career of their selected war artist. Maximum length: one page.

Background
The Canadian War Museum (please see links in the Resources section) has divided its exhibition on Canadian war art into different themes: battle (images of conflict), service (preparation and waiting for war), work (those who aren't on the front lines but contributing to the war effort), captivity/casualties (those captured during ongoing battles, and those wounded or killed) and home/leisure (what people on the home front and soldiers taking time off from war were doing).

Select
Students will select one of the above mentioned themes.

Design
Students will draw, paint, design, sketch their own visual image (painting, drawing, poster, cartoon) based on the theme they have selected.

Write
Students will write a short narrative piece, no more than two paragraphs in length, describing their visual image, what it represents, and its significance.

Present
Students will briefly present their images to the class.

EXTENSION ACTIVITY

Form
Students will be placed in groups of three or four.

Discuss
Group members will discuss with each other the visual image they have created. How do each of the images fit together? Can they tell a story?

Create
Images created by students will be combined to form a collage.

Write
Students will write accompanying text describing their collage, its meaning and significance. Maximum length: half-page.

Present
Each team will present its collage to the class and discuss its meaning and significance.

INTERMEDIATE LEVEL ACTIVITY
The War Years: Symbols of War

MATERIALS:

Art supplies, pens, paper, markers, pencils, computers with Internet access

DURATION:

Two to Three 45-minute periods

Much about war and the events surrounding war is symbolic. In the evolution of any country or society, symbols play an important role. They communicate a message and act as a standard of meaning: an image that is representative of that country. During periods of war and peace, a country's army employs objects that act as symbols: flags and heralds, and standards. Different arms boast symbols such as the configuration of the handle of a sword, or a design etched into the blade of a knife. Patches, medals and uniforms worn by military personnel, represent rank and recognition: completion of a certain course or program, performance of a heroic act or deed, fulfillment of obligations and responsibilities to attain a certain rank, etc. Wherever we look in society, we see the world filled with symbols, even if it is an icon on a computer or a text message. Within the realm of the military, and the theatre of war however, symbolism is ever present and pervasive.

OUTCOMES/EXPECTATIONS

Students will:
- Understand the sacrifice men, women, and children made in war time
- Gain appreciation for Canada's role in major conflicts overseas
- Learn about Canadian war medals, their meaning, and significance
- Learn about national symbols and their importance
- Design their own version of a war medal
- Explore the significance of national symbols
- Work cooperatively in teams
- Hone critical thinking and analytical skills

RESOURCES

www.veterans.gc.ca/eng/remembrance/medals-decorations
www.airmuseum.ca/web/ammq9911.html
www.quebecoislibre.org/010707-12.htm

www.histori.ca/peace/page.do?pageID=337
www.pch.gc.ca/progs/cpsc-ccsp/sc-cs/index_e.cfm
www.fraser.cc/FlagsCan/Nation/NatSym.html

INTRODUCTION

Discuss
Have a general discussion about symbols in our society. What is their purpose? What do they mean? Have students list as many symbols as possible on the board. Cite national symbols (flag, maple leaf, beaver, and so on) and what they represent. Do students understand their significance?

Research
Students will use the resources listed above in researching two of Canada's national symbols.

Write
Using the research conducted on the two Canadian symbols, students will write a short summary of each symbol, describing it and its significance. Maximum length: half-page.

Draw
Students will draw one of the symbols they have researched in the context it represents. This means that the symbol should not appear on its own but connected to either a flag, a plaque, a uniform, and so on.

Research
Using the resources listed above, students will research Canada's military medals and decorations.

Select
Students will select two of the military medals and decorations.

Write
Based on their research, students will write a short summary on the two military medals or decorations they selected, stating the history and significance of each. Maximum length: half page.

EXTENSION ACTIVITY

1. In 1949, the Royal Canadian Mint produced two war medals: the Defence of Britain medal and the War Medal, 1939-1945. The class will be divided into teams of two or three students. Each team will research these medals and summarize their history and significance in one page or less. The teams will then use the research and design their own war medals. The medals may

commemorate conflicts such as the First or Second World Wars, the Korean War, the Vietnam War, or even a current conflict afflicting the globe. A brief explanation of the medal's significance must be included with the concepts. Students may also create a PowerPoint presentation displaying their research and medal concepts. The medal design will then be presented to the rest of the class.

OR

2. Students, working in teams, will read *In Flanders Fields*, a poem by Colonel John McCrae, a Canadian military surgeon who served during the First World War. It is one of the most famous war poems ever written. Based on how they perceive the poem, each student team will design a commemorative medal or coin that represents John McCrae's poem. The teams will also write a description of the coin or medallion, including its meaning and significance. The designs will be presented to the rest of the class.

In Flanders Fields
By Colonel John McCrae

In Flanders fields the poppies blow
Between the crosses, row on row,
That mark our place: and in the sky
The larks still bravely singing fly
Scarce heard amid the guns below.

We are the dead: Short days ago,
We lived, felt dawn, saw sunset glow,
Loved and were loved: and now we lie
In Flanders fields!

Take up our quarrel with the foe
To you, from failing hands, we throw
The torch: be yours to hold it high
If ye break faith with us who die,
We shall not sleep, though poppies grow
In Flanders fields

SENIOR LEVEL ACTIVITY
The War Years: Reporting the War

In ancient times, war news was reported by messenger. Runners were sent by field commanders to deliver the news of a battle's outcome to an anxious ruler. Before the invention of electricity, war correspondents were sent to far-off battlefields and filed their reports via stagecoach, railroad or ship. When the battles were distant, the reports came slowly and the public received their information from newspapers that were rarely up-to-date on war events. The information was filtered through the eyes of the correspondent. Today, we live in an age of instantaneous news. Multiple news sources are available to us through a variety of media such as TV, computers and cell phones. When we receive information about combat do we think about who provides it? Do we understand what is required for war correspondents to report on dangerous and often tragic events? Should we take all the information presented to us at face value? How do we decide what to believe?

MATERIALS:

Art supplies, pens, paper, markers, pencils, computers with Internet access

DURATION:

Three to Four 45-minute periods

OUTCOMES/EXPECTATIONS

Students will:
- Understand the role of a war correspondent
- Gain appreciation for reporting during war time
- Learn how the media operate during war time
- Experiment with a variety of media to simulate war reporting
- Learn to critically assess media reports during war time
- Understand the difference between objective reporting and propaganda
- Work cooperatively in teams
- Hone critical thinking and analytical skills

RESOURCES

www.warmuseum.ca/cwm/exhibitions/newspapers/intro_e.shtml
www.warmuseum.ca/cwm/exhibitions/newspapers/information_e.shtml

ACTIVITIES

Discuss

Have a general discussion about war and war correspondents. Ask students to talk about the role of the war correspondent and its importance. Is the public well-served by the war correspondent? If so, why? If not, why not?

Research
Using the resources listed above, students will research the history and the role of the war correspondent.

Write
Students will summarize their research findings. Maximum length: one page.

Form
Students will be placed in groups of three or four.

Review
Students will track war reporting over a period of a week. This activity includes watching the news on television, scanning news on the Internet, and clipping articles from newspapers or magazines.

Report
Students will report to the group on what they saw and read over a week's time. Each group will make a list of their observations noting the type of coverage, the use of images, the use of sound, the slant of the report, the role of the reporter and the effectiveness of the reporting.

Present
Each group will make an oral presentation to the class.

EXTENSION ACTIVITY

1. Students, working in teams, will research the history of propaganda. Searching the Internet, they will select a period such as the Second World War and determine the role of propaganda in that conflict. How effective was propaganda? How did it influence civilian populations? How was propaganda used to influence public opinion? The group will put together a PowerPoint presentation for the class.

2. Student teams will write or videotape their own stories about war. The group will decide whether stories will be based on actual or fictitious events. Each team will determine what medium they will use. Print stories should be a maximum of three pages and must include photographs or illustrations. Video stories will run a maximum of two minutes and will emulate what is shown on television or the Internet. Student teams will present their war stories to the class.

UNIT 4: THE GAMES

The first documented evidence of the ancient Olympic Games stretches back almost 2300 years to 776 B.C. The games were held in a place called Olympia. The four-year interval between successive Olympic games was called an Olympiad. When referring to the Modern Olympiad, we refer not to the games themselves, but to the interval between these competitions. In effect, the Olympic Games were a substitute calendar drawing together components of Greek society every four years. These components were not part of a unified country but were city-states encompassing Italy, North Africa, and Asia Minor. The ancient games were discontinued once Greece was conquered by the Roman Empire around 146 B.C. The demise of the games resulted from a clash of philosophy. In Greek tradition, the games celebrated excellence in sport. According to Roman tradition, the games should have been a spectacle or a show designed to satisfy the audience, without emphasizing the pursuit of excellence. Finally, in 393 A.D., Emperor Theodosius I, a Christian convert, abolished the games entirely. It took 1500 years for the Olympic Games to return. In 1894, Pierre de Coubertin, of France, had a vision to re-establish the Olympic Games. Inspired by the ancient games, he founded the International Olympic Committee in Paris. Two years later, the first modern Olympic Games were held in Athens, Greece, the symbolic home of the ancient Greek games. Since that time, modern Olympic Games have grown in size and stature. The Winter Olympic Games were added, the scope of competitive sports increased, and women were permitted to compete. While their entrance into the games was, at first, granted reluctantly, some of the most impressive performances have been by women competitors in both team and solo sports events.

GENERAL OUTCOMES/EXPECTATIONS

Students will:
- Research the history of the Ancient Olympic Games and connect them to the modern version
- Explore how the modern Olympic Games differ from the ancient versions
- Understand the ability of amateur sports to affect a nation's character and pride
- Gain insight into the meaning and significance of the symbols that represent the Olympic Games
- Create their own symbols representative of the Olympic Games
- Understand more about the Olympic Games and how they operate
- Work cooperatively in teams
- Hone critical assessment and evaluation skills

KEY CONCEPTS AND ISSUES

Students will explore the significance of amateur sport and its impact and importance for the country.

JUNIOR LEVEL ACTIVITY
The Games: Celebrating Sacrifice

MATERIALS:

Art supplies, pens, paper, markers, pencils, computers with Internet access

DURATION:

Two to Four 45-minute periods

One thing we know about Olympic athletes is that they are entirely dedicated to their sport and push themselves beyond the norm to excel. In Canada, many, if not most Olympic athletes receive some form of subsidy from the federal government. Many athletes, while continuing to train for their sport, supplement that income in a variety of ways: through sponsors, family assistance, and fundraising. The Olympic Games occur every four years. During that time, athletes are in the spotlight. In the years between the Olympic Games, athletes continue to train and compete, often without public recognition. We always expect our athletes to excel and feel disappointed when they do not. It is important to recognize the commitment and dedication displayed by Olympic athletes in their quest to be best in their sport.

OUTCOMES/EXPECTATIONS

Students will:
- Research the history of the Olympic Games
- Understand the importance of amateur sport
- Appreciate the commitment and sacrifice made by Canadian Olympic athletes
- Celebrate the achievements of Canadian Olympic athletes
- Work cooperatively in teams
- Hone critical thinking and analytical skills

RESOURCES

www.olympic.org/ancient-olympic-games
www.cbc.ca/player/Sports/Olympic+Sports/ID/2462825028
www.thecanadianencyclopedia.ca/en/article/summer-olympic-games

Discuss

Introduce the topic of amateur sport into a general class discussion. If feasible, add context and background by showing a video or video footage from the opening or closing ceremonies of one of the Olympic Games. What is the difference between amateur and professional sport? See what ideas students have about this topic. Ask the class what they know about the Olympic Games. What do they think of this international competition? What are their favourite sports and who are their favourite competitors? Ask the class if they think professional athletes such as hockey, baseball, tennis or basketball players should be allowed to compete in the Olympic Games against amateur athletes. If so, why? If not, why not? List the answers on the board.

Research
Using the resource list above, students will research the history of the Olympic Games, going back to ancient times.

Summarize
Students will summarize their research in a paragraph or two.

Research
Using the resource list above, students will select one Canadian Olympic athlete and research his or her history and career.

Write
Students will write a brief profile of the athlete they've chosen, detailing his or her career and accomplishments. Maximum length: one page.

Draw
Using the profile they've written as a basis, students will draw or design a poster featuring their chosen athlete as the central image. The poster must also have a message or a theme. This theme may be tied to the promotion of the particular sport or to something that is more oriented towards public service, such as health and fitness, good nutritional choices, preserving the environment, anti-racism, and so on.

EXTENSION ACTIVITY

Students will be divided into teams of three or four. Each team member will present his or her poster design to the other team members. After completing the presentations, the team will discuss ideas for developing a public-service campaign based on the posters. How can the poster designs be used to promote an issue that the team cares about? This might involve choosing one of the posters and writing a text presentation to accompany it. If useful, the campaign can be storyboarded to provide a visual template or guideline. Or, the campaign may involve designing something completely new that reflects the needs and the interests of the team. For example, if the team is interested in the issue of global warming, they may wish to portray a skier on a hill with no snow and write accompanying text discussing the issue and why is it important. The team will need to decide who is responsible for writing, drawing, and presenting. Later, each team will present their completed campaign to the class.

INTERMEDIATE LEVEL ACTIVITY
The Games: The Public Face of Sport

MATERIALS:

Art supplies, pens, paper, markers, pencils, computers with Internet access

DURATION:

Three to Five 45-minute periods

The Olympic Games involve many countries around the world that send representative athletes to compete in a range of sports. On one level, the Olympic Games celebrate the pursuit of excellence in sport. On another level, the Olympic Games are global entertainment for millions of spectators. Every athlete wants to win. Every country wants their teams to excel. The Olympic Games are governed and controlled by the International Olympic Committee (IOC), based in Lausanne, Switzerland. The IOC was created in 1894 with the goal of resurrecting the Olympic Games, which it accomplished in 1896 when the first modern Olympic Games were held, appropriately enough, in Athens, Greece. Since 1972, each Olympic Games has had a mascot or character representative of the spirit of the competition and the theme selected by the host country.

OUTCOMES / EXPECTATIONS

Students will:
- Research the history of the Olympic games
- Understand the political aspects of the Olympic movement
- Research the concept of a mascot: what it is, and what it represents
- Choose their own mascot for an upcoming Olympic games, either summer or winter
- Make a presentation to the rest of the class
- Work cooperatively in teams
- Hone critical thinking and analytical skills

RESOURCES

www.olympic.org/ancient-olympic-games
www.thecanadianencyclopedia.ca/en/article/summer-olympic-games
www.en.wikipedia.org/wiki/International_Olympic_Committee
www.solarnavigator.net/olympic_games.htm
www.en.wikipedia.org/wiki/Mascots
www.mapsofworld.com/olympic-trivia/olympic-motto.html

Discuss

Have a general discussion with the class about the Olympic Games as a high-profile event that showcases pageantry, pomp, and theatricality in the opening and closing ceremonies. To set the context for the class, particularly for those who may never have seen the Olympic Games, provide video highlights from past Olympic Games. What does the class think about the symbols associated with the Olympic Games? For example, what do the five rings represent? Or, what does the Olympic motto, "Citius, Altius, Fortius" (Faster, Higher, Stronger) mean? Challenge students to list every Olympic mascot since 1972.

Form
Divide the class into teams of three or four.

Research
The teams will use the resource list above to research the history of the ancient and modern Olympic Games and the International Olympic Committee. This is for background information. Referring to the same resource list, the teams will also research the histories of mascots in general and mascots of the Olympic Games.

Write
The teams will provide a summary of their research findings. Maximum length: one page for each topic, two pages in total.

Brainstorm
The teams will brainstorm ideas for mascots for an upcoming Olympic Games, either summer or winter. Please note: Teams must be realistic in their options and think about what materials are easily accessible in creating their own mascot.

Draw
The teams will come up with two or three concept drawings for their designated mascot.

Finalize
After some discussion, the teams will finalize the concept they prefer.

Create
After putting the finishing touches to the mascot design of their choice, the teams will now create their mascot by bringing it to life as completely as possible, using available materials.

Present
Each of the teams will introduce their mascot to the class and describe its meaning and significance.

EXTENSION ACTIVITY

Each team will take the newly created mascot and use it as the official spokesperson for a promotional campaign. The campaign may include posters, radio, television, Internet, and/or a PowerPoint presentation. Students, who want to include television commercials in their campaign, but who lack access to video equipment, may want to present storyboards instead. This will involve conceptualizing the theme of the campaign, its purpose, intended audience, and the rationale. Teams will determine the most appropriate medium for their campaign. They must justify their choices. A written strategy of one to one-and-a-half pages must accompany the campaign. Each team will then present their Olympic mascot campaign to the rest of the class.

SENIOR LEVEL ACTIVITY
The Games: Let the Games Begin

MATERIALS:

Pens, paper, computers with Internet access

DURATION:

Six to Ten 45-minute periods

Organizing a large event like the Olympic Games requires tremendous planning, a large, active organization, and a great deal of money. Cities wishing to bid on the Olympic Games spend years and millions of dollars working on their presentations to the International Olympic Committee. Winning a bid brings enormous prestige and an opportunity to celebrate the offerings of the host city and country. Canada has hosted the Olympic Games three times: in 1976, at the Summer Olympic Games in Montreal, in 1988, at the Winter Olympic Games in Calgary and again, hosting the Winter Olympic Games in Vancouver in 2010.

OUTCOMES/EXPECTATIONS

Students will:
- Research the history of the ancient and modern Olympic Games
- Gain insight into how an event, like the Olympic Games, is organized and administered
- Understand how coins or medals are made
- Design a series of Olympic coins or medals
- Put together a strategy for marketing the Olympic coins they design
- Gain insight into the cost of organizing an event like the Olympic Games
- Conduct high-level research using the Internet
- Work cooperatively in teams
- Hone critical thinking and analytical skills

RESOURCES

www.olympic.org/ancient-olympic-games
www.thecanadianencyclopedia.ca/en/article/summer-olympic-games
www.wikipedia.org/wiki/International_Olympic_Committee
www.solarnavigator.net/olympic_games.htm
www.olympic.ca/?=winter+games+post_type=games
www.wikipedia.org/wiki/2004_Summer_Olympics
www.olympic.org/photos/sotchi-2014/opening-ceremony

ACTIVITIES

Discuss
Have a general class discussion on the Olympic Games as a significant and complex event, one that takes many years of planning and organization. If feasible, show the class some video clips or, at least, some photographs from the opening and closing ceremonies. Ask students what they think of the Olympic Games. In particular, what do they think distinguishes a successful event from an unsuccessful event?

Divide
Split the class into teams of four or five students.

Research
Using the resource list above, ask the teams to research the background and history of the Olympic Games. Have them focus on the organizational and logistical aspects of the Olympic Games, with a view to understanding how the games are organized, what is required, and the various facets that make up the Olympic Games.

Write
The teams will summarize their research in point form. Maximum length: two pages.

Brainstorm
A new series of Olympic coins is to be designed for an upcoming Olympic games, either summer or winter. The teams will brainstorm ideas and concepts for this new coin set.

Research
The teams will research the methods and processes used in designing and manufacturing coins.

Write
The teams will summarize their research on minting coins. Maximum length: two pages.

Design
The team will draft a few design concepts for the Olympic coin series.

Write
The team will write a summary of the design concept, including what the series signifies and why the particular design was selected.

Discuss
Each team will discuss and decide upon the design concepts they like best.

Finalize
The team will finalize the design concept, for their coin series.

Produce
The teams will produce a finished design for the coin series. The finished designs may be illustrated or rendered by computer, or mocked up.

Present
The teams will present the designs of their coin series to the rest of the class.

EXTENSION ACTIVITY

1. The teams will plan, develop and create the components of a promotional/marketing campaign for their coin series. They will devise a media strategy, figuring out the target market and the best way to reach this audience. The teams will also create a budget for their media plan. The plan should be very specific. For example, if the team thinks television is the best medium to use, they should put together a schedule and note the following: the stations and programs on which they wish to advertise, the number of commercials they will run, and the time period during which their commercials will appear. Teams will storyboard the campaign by illustrating the various components. They may choose to run an integrated media campaign including elements such as television, radio, print, Internet, and Podcasts. Once they finalize their campaign and detemine its elements and budget, the team will make a professional presentation to the class, who will represent a larger, more powerful audience. The "audience" will then provide feedback on the presentation.

2. The teams will revisit the research they conducted on the logistics, planning and organization of an Olympic Games competition. Each team will be given a budget of $10 million. They will allocate this budget to either the opening or closing ceremonies of an upcoming Olympic games. The teams will provide a detailed plan and budget on how this money will be spent on the ceremony they select. The budget should include items such as the venue, the entertainment, performers, music, technical requirements, security, concessions, set design and construction, lighting, maintenance, and so on. The teams will make a PowerPoint presentation to the class on their plans for these ceremonies. The presentation should be as realistic as possible, conveying images of the various elements of the chosen ceremony.

THE CANADIAN CURRENCY TIMELINE

The following timeline should be used as a reference tool. It outlines the evolution of coins and coin production in Canada. Key dates, developments and innovations are noted. A separate set of student activities accompanies the Time Line.

Early 16th Century

- Canada was inhabited by Aboriginal peoples who traded in goods on a barter basis, no currency was used
- Unusual objects like a copper shield had special economic and social value and was used by the Haidas of the west coast as a measure of wealth
- Wampum was also used to measure wealth and for gift-giving
- The wampum belt was made of small, cylindrical shells strung together, wampum also had ceremonial uses; marking peace treaties, summoning nations to war, recording important historical events and used as marks of friendship and respect
- Aboriginals traded furs for supplies with Europeans and were fond of silver objects

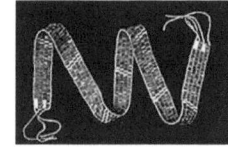

New France

1660s

- Early French colonists bartered goods, but used metal coins like the 5-sol French coin circa 1670, but there was never enough hard currency to go around
- Silver coins sent from France were taken out of circulation by merchants who used them to pay their taxes and buy European goods
- Although Spanish-American silver coins minted in Mexico sometimes came in through secret trade, the use of foreign coins was never legalized

1685

- The coin shortage grew so severe that colonial authorities resorted to using playing cards
- Playing cards were marked with the amount on the back. Cards were given to soldiers as their pay
- The practice began in 1685 and continued off and on for many years

1720

- Despite the coin shortage, playing cards were banned from being used as currency
- Colonists had to make do with a 30-deniers coin known as the "mousquetaire"
- These gold coins were meant for paying troops and civil servants, but didn't stay in circulation long

Photos: James Zagnon, National Currency Collections, Bank of Canada

1721 Gold Louis
- La Compagnie des Indes Occidentales held a monopoly over the fur trade in New France and also issued coins
- These coins were not legal tender in France and local merchants refused them
- The coin shortage remained a serious problem in the early part of the 18th century

1729 Card Money
- Due to the currency shortage, the King of France authorized a new issue of card money. Used until the fall of New France in 1760, this card money was printed on white cardboard and the size varied by denomination
- From 1720-60, other forms of paper money circulated, such as treasury bills and letters of exchange and surpassed the amount of card money in circulation

19th Century

1800s
- British colonial rule didn't solve the currency shortage. The economy still depended on the fur trade and coins from England
- Trade between the British colony and future colonies of the U.S. gave Canada additional Spanish-American dollars
- In Prince Edward Island, officials punched out the centres of these dollars and made two coins: the 5 and 1 shilling

Tokens and Army bills
- It took the public some time to trust paper money. During the War of 1812, the colonies issued army bills to finance the war effort. They circulated in large numbers and when the war ended in 1815, the British government redeemed the bills at full value. This restored trust in paper money, which led to the rise of banks
- Tokens, many of which were imported from England, served as coins during this period
- Some tokens were anonymous, that is, they didn't indicate the name of the importing merchant, while others did
- Tokens offered a discount on future purchases just like Canadian Tire money today

1821 The Rise of Banks
- In 1815, the British government redeemed army bills at full value
- Banks issued their own notes which were guaranteed by their reserves of gold and silver
- One of the first banks to receive a charter was the Montreal Bank, which changed its name to the Bank of Montreal after receiving its charter in 1822

Photos: James Zagnon, National Currency Collections, Bank of Canada

1823
- Other banks opened. The Bank of Upper Canada, opened in 1821, was for a long time the largest in the province of Canada until its collapse in 1866

1837
- Banks issued more than paper money. In the 1830s they began to import large numbers of tokens from England
- Bank of Montreal imported tokens, some anonymous and some stamped with its name
- To impose order on the issuing of tokens and purge the "junk," three banks in Montreal and the Quebec Bank issued a new series of tokens with the image of a habitant on one side and the coat of arms of Montreal and name of the bank on the other. These tokens were popularly known as Papineaus

1850s

- As trade with the United States increased, the colonies wanted to replace the sterling system, in use since 1760, with the U.S. decimal system
- Between 1853-57, the system changed over and issued coins in the 1, 5, 20, and 50 cent denominations
- Coins were minted in England since there were no minting facilities in Canada

1858
- First Canadian coinage was authorized and executed

Dominion of Canada

1867
- With the creation of the Dominion of Canada, the central government assumed responsibility for money and banking and undertook to legalize its own currency
- Ottawa issued a new series of coins in the denominations of 1, 5, 10, 25 and 50 cents
- The coins were legal tender in the four provinces that signed the Confederation Act—Ontario, Quebec, New Brunswick and Nova Scotia

1870
- Between 1868-69, the Canadian government took several mission U.S. silver coins out of circulation and exported them ensuring that only Canadian coins were used
- Waiting for the shipment of 1870 coins to arrive from England, the government issued 2 5-cent notes dubbed "shinplasters," named after similar U.S. notes that were reportedly used during the American revolution as boot liners

Photos: James Zagnon, National Currency Collections, Bank of Canada

- The government took over paper money still controlled by the banks and in 1887, Ottawa issued $1, $2, $50, $500 and $1000 notes while banks could issue notes over $4
- Some banks circumvented the agreement by issuing $6 and $7 notes and could carry out transactions without having to use the government's $1 and $2 notes. Since the Bank Act of 1871 only covered one bank, the others were free to issue their own notes in any denomination. This was changed in 1881 restricting banks to $5 notes and multiples

20th Century

1908 The First Coin

- At the opening ceremonies for the Ottawa branch of the Royal Mint on January 2, Governor General Earl Grey struck the Dominion's first domestically produced coin: a silver fifty-cent piece bearing the effigy of His Majesty King Edward VII.

1911 A Refinery

- The Ottawa Mint's Refinery is completed in January. By year's end, a record number of gold sovereigns—more than 256,000—were coined at the new facility.

A New Royal Effigy

- The effigy of His Majesty George V, who acceded to the throne in 1910, first appears on all coins minted in Canada.

1920 A Smaller Cent

- The large one-cent piece was the second coin struck by the Ottawa branch of the Royal Mint at the opening ceremonies in 1908. This large cent was replaced in 1920 by a smaller bronze coin, closer in size to its American counterpart.

1922 A Nickel of…Nickel

- Canada converts to a nickel five-cent piece to replace the more costly silver coin. Nickel is an excellent metal for coinage, and Canada is the world's leading source of nickel ore.

1930s

1931 A Truly Canadian Mint

- The Discontinuance Proclamation of December 1, 1931 transforms the Ottawa branch of the Royal Mint into the Royal Canadian Mint—a wholly Canadian institution.

1935 The First Silver Dollar

- The first silver dollar issued by the Royal Canadian Mint commemorates the silver jubilee of His Majesty King George V. The coin's reverse design, by Toronto sculptor Emanuel Hahn, portrays a Voyageur and an Aboriginal man paddling a

Photos: James Zagnon, National Currency Collections, Bank of Canada

birch-bark canoe. Faint lines in the sky represent the Northern Lights. This admirable design served for decades, an enduring reminder of Canada's early history.

1937 New Coins for Canada
- New Canadian coinage is introduced, with the effigy of the newly enthroned King George VI on the obverse (heads). Original reverse designs for the fifty-cent, twenty-five-cent, ten-cent, five-cent and one-cent coins feature Canadian emblems: the Coat of Arms, the caribou, the Bluenose fishing schooner, the beaver and the maple leaf.

1939 The Royal Visit
- A silver dollar is issued to commemorate the Royal Visit of His Majesty King George VI and Her Majesty Queen Elizabeth. The reverse design by Emanuel Hahn depicts the Centre Block and Peace Tower of the Parliament Buildings in Ottawa. The legend, Fide Suorum Regnat, means "He reigns by the faith of his people."

1940s

1943 Tombac Five Cents
- During the war years nickel was scarce, owing to its use for munitions. To conserve valuable supplies, the Royal Canadian Mint adopted tombac, a type of brass, for the five-cent piece. The coin had a twelve-sided shape to help the public distinguish it from the bronze cent. Instead of the familiar beaver, the new five-cent coin displayed the patriotic V for Victory made famous by Churchill (notice that V is also the Roman numeral for 5) and a burning torch. Designed by Thomas Shingles, Chief Engraver of the Royal Canadian Mint, the coin's rim holds a message in Morse code: "We win when we work willingly."

1948 India's Independence
- When India became independent in August of 1947, the legend IND: IMP had to be removed from the obverse of Canadian coinage, where it had appeared since 1902. An abbreviation of India Imperator, Latin for "Emperor of India," the legend was no longer appropriate. However, owing to the time required to produce new dies, the revised inscription did not appear until late in 1948.

1949 War Medals
- In honour of Canadians' gallant war service, the Defence Department commissioned the Royal Canadian Mint to strike the Defence of Britain Medal and The War Medal 1939-1945. Both medals were struck in 800 fine silver.

1949 Newfoundland Joins the Confederation
- Still considered one of Canada's most beautiful coins, the silver dollar struck to commemorate Newfoundland's entry into the Confederation depicts

Photos: James Zagnon, National Currency Collections, Bank of Canada

the "Matthew," the ship in which John Cabot made his historic discovery of Newfoundland in 1497.

1950s

1951 200th Anniversary of Nickel Discovery
- The bicentennial of the isolation and naming of nickel by Swedish chemist A.F. Cronstedt is commemorated, aptly enough, with a nickel coin: the Canadian five-cent piece. At the time of issue, Canada produced 90% of the world's nickel supply.

1953 Effigy of a Queen
- The first effigy of Her Majesty Queen Elizabeth II to appear on Canada's coins portrays the young sovereign uncrowned, her hair wreathed with laurel.

1958 Centennial of British Columbia
- This commemorative silver dollar recalls the centenary of the Caribou Gold Rush and the establishment of British Columbia as a Crown Colony. The bold reverse design by Stephen Trenka features a totem pole typical of those found among Pacific Coast Native Canadians, poised against a background of mountains.

1959 Canada's New Coat of Arms
- In 1957, the design of Canada's Coat of Arms was simplified. In addition, at the suggestion of the Queen, the crown of Edward the Confessor was substituted for that of the Tudors. The changes are reflected in this fifty-cent coin minted in 1959, which presents a new reverse modelled and engraved by Thomas Shingles.

1960s

1964 Confederation Conferences
- Fifth in the series of commemorative silver dollars, this issue recalls the centennial of Confederation conferences held in Charlottetown and Quebec City. The design is by Dinko Vodanovic of Montreal, winner of a nationwide competition. His drawing features emblems of four European nations who took part in the founding of Canada: France, Ireland, Scotland and England. More than 7 million of these popular coins were struck.

1965 A Maturing Monarch
- A new obverse sculpted by Arnold Machin portrays a more mature Elizabeth II, wearing a jewelled tiara. The legend, too, was revised: the formal Dei Gratia was reduced to D.G.

1967 Six New Reverses
- A set of six designs submitted by Canadian artist and sculptor Alex Colville were selected for new circulation coinage, minted to commemorate the 100th anniversary of the Confederation of 1867.

Photos: James Zagnon, National Currency Collections, Bank of Canada

- The coins depict common varieties of Canadian wildlife:
  - One-cent coin: A rock dove, symbol of spiritual values and peace
  - Five-cent coin: A rabbit, emblematic of fertility and new life
  - Ten-cent coin: A mackerel, to represent continuity
  - Twenty-five-cent coin: A bobcat, embodiment of intelligence and decisive action
  - Fifty-cent coin: A howling wolf, to evoke the vastness of Canada
  - Silver dollar: A Canada goose, for its dynamic serenity.
- Canadian coins reverted to their pre-1967 designs in 1968.

1968 Nickel Coinage
- As the price of silver rose, the cost of minting silver circulation coins became prohibitive. In August 1968, the Royal Canadian Mint issues the first nickel-based fifty-cent and one-dollar pieces. Smaller and darker than their silver predecessors, they are accepted with little resistance by the general public.

1969 A Crown Corporation
- Upon the recommendation of an official advisory board, and with the approval of the Government, the Royal Canadian Mint becomes a Crown Corporation on April 1, 1969. The mandate for the Crown Corporation specifically encouraged the new Board of Directors to operate the Mint as a profitable business—not simply as the supplier of a needed commodity.

1970s

1973 A Tribute to the Mounties
- The 100th anniversary of the Royal Canadian Mounted Police in 1973 is commemorated with a twenty-five-cent circulation coin and a 500 fine silver dollar collector coin that portray an RCMP officer astride his horse. The design is the work of artist Paul Cedarberg.

1976 A High-speed, High-tech Plant
- Although coin production actually started in 1975, the Winnipeg plant of the Royal Canadian Mint celebrates its official opening in 1976. All of Canada's circulation coins and coins for foreign governments are struck on the high-speed presses of this ultra-modern facility.

1976 Coins and Medals for the 21st Olympiad
- To celebrate the XXI Olympic Games in Montreal 1976, the Royal Canadian Mint launches a series of silver coins in five- and ten-dollar denominations. Seven thematic sets are produced, for a total of 28 commemorative coins, minted in both satin and proof finishes. A 100-dollar gold coin—the first-ever modern Olympic gold coin—is also struck, as well as the medals awarded to Olympic champions.

Photos: James Zagnon, National Currency Collections, Bank of Canada

1979 The Gold Maple Leaf
- In February, 1979 the Government launches the Gold Maple Leaf programme on a three-year trial basis. Distinguished by the stunning likeness of a maple leaf on its reverse, Canada's first bullion coins contained one troy ounce of twenty-four-karat gold. The Maple Leaf's success was such that Parliament authorized the coin's production on a continuing basis in 1981. Today, the Gold Maple Leaf is struck in 9999 fine gold—it's the purest gold bullion coin in the world.

1980s

1981 O Canada!
- This proof-issue 100-dollar gold coin celebrates the adoption of "O Canada" as the country's national anthem on July 1, 1980. The reverse design is by Roger Savage.

1987 Introducing the "Loonie"
- The one-dollar circulation coin is introduced as a cost-saving measure, to replace one-dollar bank notes. Minted of aureate bronze plated on pure nickel, the coin has a distinctive eleven-sided shape. The reverse presents a graceful Canadian Loon at rest on a lake, a design by one of Canada's most well-known wildlife artists, Robert-Ralph Carmichael. Since its launch, the coin has become familiarly known to Canadians as "the Loonie."

1988 Calgary Olympics
- To help finance the XV Winter Olympic Games held in Calgary, Alberta, the Royal Canadian Mint issues a series of ten commemorative sterling silver coins in proof quality only. The obverse of each coin is dated with the year of its minting, while the reverse on every coin has "Calgary 1988." The reverse designs, by various artists, feature dynamic images of athletes competing in Olympic winter sports.

Silver Maple Leaf
- Encouraged by the success of the Gold Maple Leaf programme, the Royal Canadian Mint launches the Silver Maple Leaf bullion coin in 1988. Each hand-crafted coin contains one troy ounce of 9999 fine silver.

1990s

1990 Portrait of a Queen
- The crowned effigy of Her Majesty Queen Elizabeth II that appears on Canada's coinage in 1990 shows the monarch in her 64th year. The portrait is the work of Dora de Pedery-Hunt, the first Canadian to design a royal effigy for Canadian coinage. It remained in use until 2003.

1996 The Patented Bi-metallic Coin
- The two-dollar coin is introduced on February 19, 1996 to replace the two-dollar bank note—as coins last some 20 times longer than notes. Familiarly known as

Photos: James Zagnon, National Currency Collections, Bank of Canada

the "Toonie," the two-dollar coin features a distinctive bi-metallic locking mechanism engineered and patented by the Royal Canadian Mint. The coin's outer ring is nickel; the inner core is aluminum bronze (92% copper, 6% aluminum, 2% nickel). In 1996 alone, 375 million "Toonies" are struck at the Royal Canadian Mint's Winnipeg plant—an amazing feat.
- The reverse depicts an adult polar bear in early summer on an ice floe. It was designed by Ontario artist Brent Townsend, who specializes in studies of North American wildlife and landscapes.

1997 A New Round Cent
- The familiar one-cent coin contained 98% copper until 1997, when its composition is modified. The Canadian penny—the workhorse of our circulation coinage—is now made of copper-plated zinc. The twelvesided form proves difficult to plate, resulting in the reintroduction of the round design.

1999 Coins for the Millennium
- To mark the end of the second millennium, the Royal Canadian Mint strikes a different twenty-five-cent coin design for each month of 1999 and 2000. The artwork is chosen from more than 66,000 entries submitted by Canadians from all walks of life, as part of the Mint-sponsored "Create a Centsation! coin design contest. The 1999 series looks back on the preceding thousand years; the 2000 coins look forward to the future.

- The Millennium programme is hugely successful, making coin collectors of millions of Canadians. The Mint produces over 500 million twenty-five-cent coins during 1999 and 2000 to keep up with demand.

A New Dimension in Design
- The Royal Canadian Mint celebrates the 20th anniversary of its signature Gold Maple Leaf with a high-tech version of the bullion coin, featuring a beautiful maple leaf hologram. It is a first for the Mint, and a clear demonstration of technical prowess. The innovation consists in striking the hologram directly onto the coin's surface, instead of producing and applying it in separate steps.

2000s

First Coloured Collector Coin
- "Celebration," a twenty-five-cent piece designed for the Millennium programme, is the first Canadian coin ever to be re-issued in a colourized version. Released in July 2000, this special collector version features a Canadian flag with a red maple leaf and side panels.

2001 Multi-Ply Plating
- With the development of a patented multi-ply plating technique, the Royal Canadian Mint steps once again to the forefront of minting technologies.

Photos: James Zagnon, National Currency Collections, Bank of Canada

In 2001, Canadian circulation coinage converts to this moneysaving production method. The five-, ten-, twenty-five- and fifty-cent coins are struck on nickel-plated steel blanks; a copper-plated steel blank is used for the one-cent piece. Multi-ply technology is one of several major innovations from the Mint. Others include selective plating and laser enhancement, technologies used for collector coins.

2003 Updated Royal Effigy

- Introduced a year after the Golden Jubilee of Her Royal Majesty Queen Elizabeth II, the latest obverse effigy depicts the Queen without a crown. The portrait was designed by Suzanna Blount.

2004 Lest We Forget

- The Royal Canadian Mint releases the world's first coloured circulation coin commemorating the Poppy, Canada's flower of remembrance. The twenty-five-cent piece presents a stylized red poppy on the reverse.
- The coin is dedicated to all of the 117,000 gallant Canadians who gave their lives while in the nation's service. To meet the engineering and design challenges involved in producing this innovative coin, the Mint perfected a high-speed colouring process that can generate 30 million coins. The process ensures that the colour adheres to the metal and resists day-to-day wear.

2005

- In celebration of the Year of the Veteran and the 60th Anniversary of the Allied victory in the Second World War, four coins and coin sets were introduced. These were the five-cent sterling silver coin and medallion set depicting VE Day Celebrations; the five-dollar silver coin depicting the 60th Anniversary of the end of the Second World War; the 50-cent sterling silver six coin set also marking the end of the Second World War; and the Brilliant Uncirculated Coin Set with a 25-cent sterling silver coin and eight brilliant uncirculated Euro coins and a commemorative Royal Dutch medallion. The coins are dedicated to 60 years of liberation highlighting the special relationship between Canada and the Netherlands
- 25th anniversary of Terry Fox's Marathon of Hope—a journey to raise funds for cancer research. A one-dollar coin is issued, featuring the image of Terry Fox, the first Canadian-born individual to be highlighted on a circulation coin
- 25-cent coins celebrating the Saskatchewan and Alberta centennials. For the first time in its history, the Royal Canadian Mint offered the public an opportunity to vote for a coin design. Designs were created by artists representing each province.
- Saluting Canada's Veterans, a commemorative 25-cent coin was struck. Up to 30 million coins were produced

Photos: James Zagnon, National Currency Collections, Bank of Canada

2006
- The one-dollar "Lucky Loonie" features the Olympic logo. It was unveiled four years after a Loonie was secretly buried at centre ice during the 2002 Winter Olympic Games when the Canadian men's and women's hockey teams skated to gold
- The world's second colour circulation coin was unveiled to promote breast cancer awareness. The 25-cent coin featured the distinctive pink ribbon
- The 10th anniversary of the two-dollar coin or "Toonie" featured a "Name the Bear" contest
- A new Mint mark, symbol of the Royal Canadian Mint's reputation for high quality and innovation, was added to all circulation coins on the obverse (heads) side depicting Queen Elizabeth II.

2011
- The Bank of Canada began issuing polymer bills.

2013
- The penny is phased out of circulation. In February 2013, the Royal Canadian Mint struck its last one cent coin.

Photos: James Zagnon, National Currency Collections, Bank of Canada

TIMELINE ACTIVITIES

The following set of activities are connected to the timeline.
The activities explore a range of topics that are currency and money-related.

Master of the Mint
Students will undertake research online to determine the role of the Master of the Mint, what it is he/she does and its importance.

Barter
Before Canada, or any country had a formal system of currency, barter or trading goods for goods or goods for services, came into being. That is, beaver pelts for grain, sacks of corn for tools and so on. Students will research the history of barter and write a short report one page in length.

www.pbs.org/wgbh/nova/moolah/history.html
www.ex.ac.uk/~RDavies/arian/barter.html
www.funsocialstudies.learninghaven.com/articles/bartering.htm
www.esty.ancients.info/numis/index.html

Credit
We hear a lot about the availability of credit, but many of us really don't understand what it means or how to use credit in a responsible manner. Students, using the resources directly below, will research the history of credit. They will make a presentation to the class that clearly demonstrates how credit works within our economy.

www.pbs.org/wgbh/pages/frontline/shows/credit
www.wikipedia.org/wiki/Credit_history
www.inventors.about.com/od/mstartinventions/a/money.htm

Debit
Just as credit is an important economic tool in our society, the use of debit cards has mushroomed in Canada. Students will research online the issue of debit and debit cards and report their findings to the class.

www.wikipedia.org/wiki/Debit_card

Math and coins
Please see the resources below for some fun and informative activities involving mathematics and coins.

www.aaamath.com/B/mny.htm
www.lessonplanspage.com/MathDistinguishingCoinsAndTheirValue2.htm
www.illinoisearlylearning.org/tipsheets/coins.htm
www.cyberbee.com/probability/mathprob.html

Coin Production

Coins have been made in various forms for thousands of years. Over the centuries, the processes and technologies have improved dramatically. The Royal Canadian Mint is among the most innovative manufacturers of quality coins in the world.

Students will research the history of coin production and create a presentation documenting how coins from a given period are produced. Younger students may create their own drawings or illustrations while older students may use a presentation program like PowerPoint.

www.coin-gallery.com/cgearlycoins.htm
www.worldcoincatalog.com/Contents/Invention/invention.htm
www.britishmuseum.org/explore/highlights/highlight_objects/cm/s/silver_decadrachm.aspx

Coin Flipping

Coin tossing or coin flipping has become part of our culture. We see that, on occasion, some large decisions may be based on the flip of a coin. In professional sports, such as football, a coin is tossed to determine who starts the game on offence or defence. Sometimes when we are undecided about certain things, a coin may be tossed to settle a dispute. Students will research the topic of coin tossing and may go through a set of math-based activities involving the coin toss while exploring the field of probability.

www.wikipedia.org/wiki/Coin_flipping
www.mathworld.wolfram.com/CoinTossing.html

Value of Money

It is important for everyone to know the value of money but we can and do forget. The resources below will give an historical perspective on this issue as well as a means to convert one currency to another. Teachers may wish to try out these activities with their class.

www.ex.ac.uk/~RDavies/arian/current/howmuch.html
www.investopedia.com/articles/03/082703.asp
www.coins.nd.edu/ColCurrency/CurrencyIntros/IntroValue.html
www.x-rates.com/calculator.html
www.vancouver.hm/money.html

Counterfeiting

As we know, coins and money have tremendous allure. So much so, that some enterprising but misguided individuals try to produce fake coins or bills. As technologies become more sophisticated, however, it is sometimes difficult to tell counterfeit banknotes, from the real thing. Have students research the topic of counterfeiting. They should know that the act of counterfeiting is illegal when fake money or coins are used to attempt legitimate transactions. Law enforcement has become more sophisticated in detecting these false items. Students will research the history of counterfeiting and write a short report and present it to the class.

www.wikipedia.org/wiki/Counterfeit
www.cbc.ca/player/Shows/Shows/Doc+Zone/2012-13/ID/2324420977

Online banking

Not too long ago, anyone with a bank account went into a branch to conduct transactions. Now, all of this can be done electronically. Students will research the phenomenon of online banking to better understand how it evolved. After having completed this preliminary research, the class will be divided into groups of four or five. Each group will discuss both the pros and cons of online banking. For example, online banking provides convenience, you can bank at your leisure late at night or during the day without having to stand in line. On the other hand, it reduces the amount of social interaction a person may have and increases our reliance on technology. The student groups will report the outcome of their discussions to the rest of the class.

www.gahtan.com/alan/articles/ibank-a.htm
www.wikipedia.org/wiki/Online_banking

Identity Theft

One of the consequences of having a banking system online is the potential for fraud and other criminal activities. An illegal activity that has been mentioned in the media is identity theft. What is it? How does it occur? How can it be prevented? How do you get your identity back? Students will research this area and list a series of recommendations as to how to safeguard and protect against this illegal activity. Students will be placed in groups of three or four and will storyboard a television commercial that generates awareness about identity theft.

Each group will present its story board to the rest of the class.

www.cmcweb.ca/eic/site/cmc-cmc.nsf/eng/fe00078.html
www.rcmp-grc.gc.ca/scams-fraudes/index-eng.htm
www.cmcweb.ca/epic/internet/incmc-cmc.nsf/en/fe00084e.html

Canadian Money is different

How and why is Canadian money different? Is this a good thing? Is it important to have money that is distinctive? If so, what does it say about the country? Students will have a general discussion on this topic in class.

www.wikipedia.org/wiki/Canadian_dollar
www.reference.com/browse/wiki/Canadian_dollar
www.wikipedia.org/wiki/Identity_theft

Future of money?

Does money have a future? For all of the techno-gadgets that exist in society today and the access to technology, do we actually need hard currency? Is there a better way? The class as a whole will conduct research to flesh out this topic. The class will be given a debating question. There will be two teams, the pro side and the con side. Each side will present its case in a lively, energetic and creative fashion. No holds barred. The rest of the class will sit as judges and vote for the team that made the most compelling and believable case.

www.wikipedia.org/wiki/Electronic_money

= LESSON FIVE

STAR TREK
WHAT HAS IT TAUGHT US ABOUT HUMANITY?

Popular media present an excellent means to explore difficult and meaningful moral and ethical issues. The sci-fi genre, in particular, has, through imaginative scenarios and storylines, exposed often difficult and serious issues in a creative way. One example of this is the original Star Trek television series broadcast in the years 1966-1969. It is the basis for the entire Star Trek oeuvre including the Star Trek films and various spinoff television series such as Star Trek: Next Generation, Star Trek: Voyager and Star Trek: Deep Space Nine among others.

GRADE LEVEL:
6 - 9

CURRICULA THEMES:

Media Literacy, Literacy, Social Studies, Language Arts

LEARNING OUTCOMES

Students will:
- Explore the use of different media formats such as storyboards, video and interactive media as learning tools
- Gain insight into how media can be used to promote a specific perspective or point of view
- Understand how popular media like a television series such as Star Trek explores important ethical issues
- Create visual and oral presentations of their work
- Work collaboratively in teams
- Hone critical assessment and evaluation skills
- Develop online research skills
- Create work using available new media tools and resources

INTRODUCTION

Although Star Trek's main purpose was entertainment for its television audience, the show did not shy away from exposing important issues and themes. Within this lesson plan, students will research issues raised by a given episode of the Star Trek television series and develop their own media tools that express a specific moral perspective.

Students, working in teams will develop, in a progressive way, increasingly sophisticated media resources. Teachers should impress upon them that they are creating relevant media content corresponding to a specific theme, and students need to think about and understand the impact they want their media resources to have on the audience and user base.

CURRICULUM LINKS

GRADE 6 MEDIA LITERACY

Overall Expectations

By the end of Grade 6, students will:
- Demonstrate an understanding of a variety of media texts
- Identify some media forms and explain how the conventions and techniques associated with them are used to create meaning
- Create a variety of media texts for different purposes and audiences, using appropriate forms, conventions, and techniques
- Reflect on and identify their strengths as media interpreters and creators, areas for improvement, and the strategies they found most helpful in understanding and creating media texts

GRADE 7 MEDIA LITERACY

Overall Expectations

By the end of Grade 7, students will:
- Demonstrate an understanding of a variety of media texts
- Identify some media forms and explain how the conventions and techniques associated with them are used to create meaning
- Create a variety of media texts for different purposes and audiences, using appropriate forms, conventions, and techniques
- Reflect on and identify their strengths as media interpreters and creators, areas for improvement, and the strategies they found most helpful in understanding and creating media texts

GRADE 8 MEDIA LITERACY

Overall Expectations

By the end of Grade 8, students will:
- Demonstrate an understanding of a variety of media texts
- Identify some media forms and explain how the conventions and techniques associated with them are used to create meaning
- Create a variety of media texts for different purposes and audiences, using appropriate forms, conventions, and techniques
- Reflect on and identify their strengths as media interpreters and creators, areas for improvement, and the strategies they found most helpful in understanding and creating media texts

ACTIVITY ONE
The Media Morality Play: Storyboarding

Students will work in teams of three or four.

Background

Students will use the Internet to research the classic episode of the original Star Trek series: "Let That Be Your Last Battlefield" (www.wikipedia.org/wiki/Let_That_Be_Your_Last_Battlefield, http://memory-alpha.org/en/wiki/Let_That_Be_Your_Last_Battlefield), or an episode from the original Star Trek series or a subsequent Star Trek series of their choice.

MATERIALS:

Devices with Internet access, pads of paper or drawing pad, markers, pens and/or design/layout software.

DURATION:

Four to Five 45-minute periods

In the selected episode, students will:
- Describe the plot line of the episode. One to two paragraphs.
- What is the core conflict in the plot? One paragraph.
- Who are the main characters? Make a list with a brief description.
- What are the root causes of the core conflict? One paragraph.
- Is the theme of the episode relevant today? If so, why? One to two paragraphs.
- Is the core conflict in the episode resolved? If so, how? One paragraph.

The answers to the above will be discussed or presented within each group during class time then handed in to the teacher for assessment.

Instructions

Students will create a storyboard based on a scenario involving the two main characters from the online graphic novel, The Canadian Northern Project (*www.teachmag.com/cnp*)

Resources

www.youtube.com/watch?v=e-yeI83fN6s
www.usabilitynet.org/tools/storyboarding.htm
www.suite.io/tammy-andrew/1yzz21q

- Review the resources listed above that detail the basics in creating a storyboard if students have not done this before. There are also a wide range of online resources available through searching the phrase 'creating a storyboard' online.
- As mentioned in the introduction, Alex and ZaZi are confronted with an ethical dilemma in the Canadian Northern Project interactive graphic novel. Also, "Let That Be Your Last Battlefield" explores the topic of racism in a creative but dramatic way. For the storyboard, students will develop a storyline using the characters of Alex and ZaZi to explore a topic that deals with a strong moral or ethical issue of the student team's choosing.
- Students will write a brief script that they will storyboard. The script should entail a sequence of "shots" that add up to a maximum of five minutes of running time.
- Referring to the resources above, student teams will create their storyboard.
- Once the storyboards have been completed, each student team will present theirs to the rest of the class.
- After the presentations have been made, if there is time, initiate a discussion on what was learned about the storyboarding process and how effective storyboards are for exploring important ethical and moral topics.

ACTIVITY TWO
The Media Morality Play: Shooting Video

Students will work in teams of three or four.

Background

Following are some resources to provide insight into shooting video for a classroom project:

www.guardian.co.uk/lifeandstyle/2008/jan/26/makingvideo.techniques4
www.solutionwatch.com/326/eyespot-shoot-mix-and-share-your-video
www.kidsvid.altec.org/nav_pages/teaching.html
www.youthlearn.org/activities/you-oughta-be-pictures-introduction-making-videos
http://picturethis.sdcoe.net

Instructions

Referring to the above resources on video development and production, student teams will video the storyboard they created in the first activity. The video should be a maximum length of five minutes.

- Students will flesh out their scripts for the video they are going to produce
- Student teams may use a variety of genres or formats for the video they wish to produce, for example, live action, animation, claymation and so on
- Student teams will shoot and edit the video
- Once completed, student teams will present their video to the rest of the class and explain briefly what the video is about, how it was produced, and its purpose
- Students will then be asked to write, in a paragraph or two, how the video they produced developed the ethical/moral theme and how this was enhanced by the video production

MATERIALS:

Computers with Internet access, video/editing software such as iMovie, Final Cut Pro or other PC-based video/editing software such as Windows Movie Maker, smartphone or camcorder with audio recording capability and accessories.

DURATION:

Four to Five 45-minute periods

MATERIALS:

Devices with Internet access, video/editing software, smartphone or camcorder, website development software.

DURATION:

Three to Five 45-minute periods

ACTIVITY THREE:
The Morality Play Part Three: Going Interactive

Students will work in teams of three or four.

Background

www.scratch.mit.edu (Interactive tools and resources developed by the M.I.T. Multimedia Lab)

http://enhancinged.wgbh.org/kids/formats/web/elements.html (Interactive applications developed by PBS, the public broadcasting service in the United States)

(Interactive music lesson developed by PBS)
www.pbs.org/wnet/musicinstinct/education/lesson-1-experimental-music/lesson-overview/81

www.interactivemultimediatechnology.blogspot.com/2006/04/updated-52006-interactive-multimedia.html (Listing of interactive media projects and lesson plans)

www.apple.com/education/ipad (A guide to using the iPad for education)

Instructions

- Using the video created in Activity Two, students will develop interactive online resources with the video as the key component
- This means developing a website using the video clip they've created. The website will become a discussion forum for the ethical issue that has been explored in the video clip
- Potential elements of the website may include social media feeds, blogs, wiki application, links to relevant resources on the ethical issue, educational resources if applicable, historical content, games, and apps
- Students will divide up the roles and responsibilities for the Web development (the site can be relatively simplistic based on time allotted and student capability—at the discretion of the teacher), and set a timeline for development
- Once the website is posted to the school or class server, student teams will develop an oral presentation that describes their site to the rest of the class

EVALUATION AND ASSESSMENT

General

Discussion

Level 1   Did not participate or contribute to the teacher-directed discussions
Level 2   Participated somewhat in the teacher-directed discussions
Level 3   Actively participated in the teacher-directed discussions
Level 4   Made a significant contribution to the teacher-directed discussions

Content

Level 1   Demonstrated limited understanding of concepts, facts, and terms
Level 2   Demonstrated some understanding of concepts, facts, and terms
Level 3   Demonstrated considerable understanding of concepts, facts, and terms
Level 4   Demonstrated thorough understanding of concepts, facts, and terms

Written Work

Level 1   Written report had many grammatical errors, was poorly structured and confusing
Level 2   Written report was generally clear, but has numerous grammatical errors
Level 3   Written report was well-structured and clear, but has a few significant/ grammatical errors
Level 4   Written report was very clear, well-organized with few errors

Oral Presentation

Level 1   Oral report was confusing, lacked emphasis and energy, with no discussion resulting
Level 2   Oral report was clear, but lacked emphasis and energy, with little discussion resulting
Level 3   Oral report was clear and vibrantly presented, but lacked some emphasis and energy, with a good discussion resulting
Level 4   Oral report was clear and enthusiastically presented, with energetic discussion resulting

Teamwork

Level 1   1 or 2 members dominated the team, very little co-operation
Level 2   Majority of the group made a contribution with some recognition of individual strengths, but co-operation was superficial
Level 3   Most members made a significant contribution, with a good level of co-operation
Level 4   All members made a significant contribution, individual strengths were recognized and used effectively, excellent co-operation among group members

Specific

Ethical/Moral Issues

Level 1   Student had little insight or understanding of the relevance of ethical issues and the use of media tools and resources

Level 2 Student had basic insight or understanding of the relevance of ethical issues and the use of media tools and resources

Level 3 Student had good insight or understanding of the relevance of ethical issues and the use of media tools and resources

Level 4 Student had excellent insight or understanding of the relevance of ethical issues and the use of media tools and resources

Activity 1

Level 1 Student made little effort and had little understanding of storyboards and media literacy

Level 2 Student made basic effort and had some basic understanding of storyboards and media literacy

Level 3 Student made significant effort and had good understanding of storyboards and media literacy

Level 4 Student made excellent effort and had exemplary understanding of storyboards and media literacy

Activity 2

Level 1 Student made little effort and had little understanding of video and its relevance to media literacy

Level 2 Student made some effort and had some understanding of video and its relevance to media literacy

Level 3 Student made good effort and had good understanding of video and its relevance to media literacy

Level 4 Student made exemplary effort and had excellent understanding of video and its relevance to media literacy

Activity 3

Level 1 Student made little effort and had little interest in the development of interactive media tools

Level 2 Student made some effort and had some interest in the development of interactive media tools

Level 3 Student made good effort and had an active interest in the development of interactive media tools

Level 4 Student made an excellent effort and had an enthusiastic interest in the development of interactive media tools

LESSON SIX

STELLAR ARTS
HOW THE UNIVERSE INSPIRES CREATIVITY

Humans have always been fascinated with the night sky. Most of us gaze up at the stars and constellations with some awe. Sights such as the aurora borealis inspire feelings of wonder. For millennia, stars in the sky have formed the basis of mythology, religion, and art. The stars and constellations have been named and those names are infused with meaning and symbolism. Many artists and scientists have looked to the night sky for motivation and a spark to fire up their creativity. Not much has changed since ancient times. Contemporary artists and scientists still look to the night sky to help them solve a problem or create a work of art.

GRADE LEVEL:
6 – 9

CURRICULA THEMES:

Social Studies,
Language Arts,
Visual Arts,
Science

A Halo for NGC 6164
Image Credit & Copyright: Martin Pugh & Rick Stevenson

THE GOLD BOOK OF LESSON PLANS: VOLUME ONE

INTRODUCTION

Students will explore the creative elements that the universe has inspired in artists throughout history. They will create their own works of art based on ideas generated through exploring myths and mythology, stars, planets, and constellations.

LEARNING OUTCOMES

Students will:
- Gain insight into the history of myths and mythology
- Connect mythology to creative expression
- Learn about constellations, planets, and stars
- Create a work of art inspired by the universe
- Develop the work of art into an interactive/multimedia project
- Explore the mythology of other cultures
- Enhance social skills by working in teams
- Use critical thinking skills to solve problems and meet challenges

CURRICULUM CONNECTIONS

VISUAL ARTS (GRADES 6-8)

Overall Expectations

Creating and Presenting: apply the creative process to produce art works in a variety of traditional two-and three-dimensional forms, as well as multimedia art works, that communicate feelings, ideas, and understandings using elements, principles, and techniques of visual arts, as well as current media technologies.

Reflecting, Responding, and Analyzing: apply the critical analysis process to communicate feelings, ideas, and understandings in response to a variety of art works and art experiences.

Exploring Forms and Cultural Contexts: demonstrate an understanding of a variety of art forms, styles, and techniques from the past and present, and their socio-cultural and historical contexts.

Oral Communication (Grades 6-8)

Students will:
- Listen in order to understand and respond appropriately in a variety of situations for a variety of purposes

- Use speaking skills and strategies appropriately to communicate with different audiences for a variety of purposes
- Reflect on and identify their strengths as listeners and speakers, areas for improvement, and the strategies they found most helpful in oral communication situations

Reading

Students will:
- Read and demonstrate an understanding of a variety of literary, graphic, and informational texts, using a range of strategies to construct meaning
- Recognize a variety of text forms, text features, and stylistic elements, and demonstrate understanding of how they help communicate meaning
- Use knowledge of words and cueing systems to read fluently
- Reflect on and identify their strengths as readers, areas for improvement, and the strategies they found most helpful before, during, and after reading

Writing

Students will:
- Generate, gather, and organize ideas and information to write for an intended purpose and audience
- Draft and revise their writing, using a variety of informational, literary, and graphic forms and stylistic elements appropriate for the purpose and audience
- Use editing, proofreading, and publishing skills and strategies, and knowledge of language conventions, to correct errors, refine expression, and present their work effectively
- Reflect on and identify their strengths as writers, areas for improvement, and the strategies they found most helpful at different stages in the writing process

Media Literacy

Students will:
- Demonstrate an understanding of a variety of media texts
- Identify some media forms and explain how the conventions and techniques associated with them are used to create meaning
- Create a variety of media texts for different purposes and audiences, using appropriate forms, conventions, and techniques
- Reflect on and identify their strengths, areas for improvement, and the strategies they found most helpful in understanding and creating media texts

BACKGROUND INFORMATION

http://neave.com/planetarium

Downloadable star chart poster of the Northern Hemisphere
www.armaghplanet.com/pdf/BT_PDF/star_chart_poster.pdf

Images captured with the Hubble telescope
http://hubblesite.org/gallery/album/star
http://heritage.stsci.edu/gallery/gallery.html

Ancient Greek mythology
www.ancientgreece.com/s/Mythology

Modern Art and Mythology
https://suite.io/meg-nola/1r802fk

Greek mythology in western art and literature
http://en.wikipedia.org/wiki/Greek_mythology_in_western_art_and_literature

NASA Quest Challenges for students
http://quest.arc.nasa.gov

Article on virtual environments in the classroom
http://studiowikitecture.wordpress.com/2008/10/17/wikitecture-40-re-inventing-the-virtual-classroom

ACTIVITY ONE

MATERIALS:

Computers, tablets, or mobile devices with Internet access. Drawing and writing materials, Design/illustration software

DURATION:

Two to Three 45-minute periods

Students will begin to plan a work of art based on a mythological figure represented by a star or constellation in the sky by investigating and researching different approaches and styles of art.

Instructions

- Students will access the links above or ones they have found on their own to examine and explore star charts
- From the star charts students have examined, they will select a star, constellation, or planet named after a mythological character
- Students will research the mythological character and write a brief description (up to two paragraphs)
- Students will write an original short story based on the mythological character they have selected, roughly one page in length

- Select one of the following modern artistic movements: Cubism, Impressionism, Abstract, Pointillism, or Surrealism and research its history describing the approach and philosophy to painting, art, and life in an essay of about two pages in length
- Students will find an image that uses the universe as the basis for its inspiration in the style of the modern artistic movement they have selected
- Students will describe in a paragraph or two the style of the image pointing out how and why it belongs to the artistic movement selected, and why and how they think the image inspired the artist

Note: The image can be a photograph, digital image, etc., as well as a sculpture or painting.

ACTIVITY TWO

Students will create a work of art based on a mythological figure.

Instructions

- Students will do a series of preliminary sketches of their work of art based on the mythological figure they've researched in the previous activity
- The piece of art may appear in one or more formats, e.g., painting, sculpture, digital image, photograph, collage, mosaic, etc. The style of art may also be one selected from the activity above, i.e., abstract, cubist, impressionist, etc.
- Materials used are open-ended and may include: oil paint, acrylics, water colours, plaster, stone, wire, Plasticine, paper mâché, beads, etc. Interpretation of the mythological figure forms part of the artistic process and may appear as realistic or not, as long as the student can provide a rationale and explanation for their approach to the work
- Students will work on and complete their piece of art
- Students will write a description of their piece of art detailing what it is, their approach, and how it links to a star, constellation, or planet
- Students will present their work of art to other members of the class

MATERIALS:

Computers, tablets, or mobile devices with Internet access Drawing and writing materials. Design/illustration programs or apps Art materials, as required.

DURATION:

Two to Three 45-minute periods

ACTIVITY THREE

MATERIALS:

Computers, tablets, or mobile devices with Internet access Drawing and writing materials, Design/illustration programs, websites, or apps, Digital camera or device with a camera, Web design programs, websites, or apps

DURATION:

Three to Four 45-minute periods

Students will work in teams to incorporate their work of art into a multimedia/interactive project

Instructions

- Students will work in groups and decide if they want to develop their multimedia/interactive project around one, some, or all of the works of art they created in the previous activity
- Student teams will determine what format the multimedia/interactive project will take and then break out the steps required and the roles and responsibilities of the team members
- Student teams will design, then build their multimedia/interactive project
- Student teams will write a detailed description of their multimedia/interactive project
- Student teams will present their multimedia/interactive projects to the rest of the class using appropriate presentation tools and/or software

EVALUATION AND ASSESSMENT

General

Discussion

Level 1   Did not participate or contribute to the teacher-directed discussions
Level 2   Participated somewhat in the teacher-directed discussions
Level 3   Actively participated in the teacher-directed discussions
Level 4   Significantly contributed to the teacher-directed discussions

Content

Level 1   Demonstrated limited understanding of concepts, facts, and terms
Level 2   Demonstrated some understanding of concepts, facts, and terms
Level 3   Demonstrated considerable understanding of concepts, facts, and terms
Level 4   Demonstrated thorough understanding of concepts, facts, and terms

Written Work

Level 1   Written report had many grammatical errors and was poorly structured and confusing
Level 2   Written report was adquate, but had numerous grammatical errors
Level 3   Written report was well-structured and clear, but had a few significant/grammatical errors
Level 4   Written report was very clear, well-organized and had few errors

Oral Presentation

Level 1 Oral report was confusing, lacked emphasis and energy, with no discussion resulting

Level 2 Oral report was adequate, but lacked emphasis and energy with little discussion resulting

Level 3 Oral report was clear, but lacked some emphasis and energy with a good discussion resulting

Level 4 Oral report was clear and enthusiastically presented, with engaged discussion resulting

Teamwork

Level 1 One or two members dominated the team, very little co-operation

Level 2 Majority of the group made a contribution with some recognition of individual strengths, but co-operation was superficial

Level 3 Most members made a significant contribution, with a good level of co-operation

Level 4 All members made a significant contribution, individual strengths were recognized and used effectively, excellent co-operation among group members

Specific

Activity 1

Level 1 Student made little effort and had little understanding of mythology and accepted schools of art and painting

Level 2 Student made basic effort and had some basic understanding of mythology and accepted schools of art and painting

Level 3 Student made significant effort and had good understanding of mythology and accepted schools of art and painting

Level 4 Student made excellent effort and had exemplary understanding of mythology and accepted schools of art and painting

Activity 2

Level 1 Student made little effort to create a work of art based on a mythological figure

Level 2 Student made some effort to create a work of art based on a mythological figure

Level 3 Student made a good effort to create a work of art based on a mythological figure

Level 4 Student made an exemplary effort to create a work of art based on a mythological figure

Activity 3

Level 1—Student made little effort and had little interest in the development of an interactive/multimedia project
Level 2—Student made some effort and had some interest in the development of an interactive/multimedia project
Level 3—Student made good effort and had an active interest in the development of an interactive/multimedia project
Level 4—Student made an excellent effort and had an enthusiastic interest in the development of an interactive/multimedia project

LESSON SEVEN

THE HUMAN RIGHTS PROJECT

This teaching unit will allow teachers and students to explore in detail the issues surrounding human rights with a particular emphasis on the plight of refugees. They will understand that along with rights come a set of key responsibilities.

GRADE LEVEL:
6 – 12

CURRICULA THEMES:

History, Geography, Language Arts, Political Science, Media Studies, Music and Social Studies

Excerpt from the Preamble to the 1948 Universal Declaration of Human Rights (UDHR):

"Whereas recognition of the inherent dignity and of the equal and inalienable rights of all members of the human family is the foundation of freedom, justice and peace in the world...

Whereas disregard and contempt for human rights have resulted in barbarous acts which have outraged the conscience of mankind, and the advent of a world in which human beings shall enjoy freedom of speech and belief and freedom from fear and want has been proclaimed as the highest aspiration of the common people...

Whereas it is essential, if man is not to be compelled to have recourse, as a last resort, to rebellion against tyranny and oppression, that human rights should be protected by the rule of law..."

The United Nations drafted the Universal Declaration of Human Rights in 1948. It was the first time such rights were articulated and drafted into law. It was also the first time an attempt had been made to regulate how states treated their own citizens. The Declaration now celebrates its 66th anniversary. Some 125 states are signatories to the Declaration and/or succeeding covenants and protocols. It is fair to say that the Declaration has had a profound effect on public policy for some and in particular, for Canada. There is a clear connection between UDHR and the Canadian Charter of Rights and Freedoms, for example.

Although Canada's record with regard to human rights and refugees in particular, is not perfect by any means, overall the country is cited as one of the leaders in the field and a model for others to follow. In 1986, Canada was awarded the Nansen Medal in recognition of "the major and sustained contribution made by the People of Canada to the cause of refugees." Even in the best of cases, however, there is always room for improvement. Why then is it important to raise the issues of human rights and refugees for Canadians? Those of us who have lived here for some time, perhaps generations, may have little knowledge or experience with human rights abuses. We may have no first-hand knowledge of the disruption, the terror, or the upheaval experienced by refugees who come to this country seeking safety and security. We may have no knowledge of the labyrinthine processes they must navigate to become citizens or receive official refugee status. Some succeed. Those who fail may be returned to a hostile region where their lives are endangered. We, those of us who are removed from the world of refugees, may have become complacent with regard to our status as citizens. Take it for granted. Students in school may not even be aware of these issues or that these issues have faces not unlike theirs. Faces that register pain, hunger, and uncertainty. Wide-eyed faces that look for understanding and recognition from others. Passionate faces that desire a chance to succeed and live a life free from danger, united with their families. Students may not realize that for many around the world, Canada is viewed as a haven, a sanctuary that can deliver the safety and security refugees seek. Canada can and should lead by example and show "the content of its character."

LEARNING OUTCOMES

Students will:
- Appreciate the significance of the Universal Declaration of Human Rights
- Learn about the key human rights issues for refugees
- Understand the relationship between refugee rights and other important international conventions on human rights.
- Examine how the UDHR has inspired the Canadian Charter of Rights and Freedoms and the special meaning that these rights have for refugees in Canada
- Understand the importance of legislation for protecting human rights
- Critically analyze Canadian refugee policies during the 20th century
- Develop a personal sense of value and concept of justice and equality
- Explore the role of the media in its coverage of refugee and human rights issues in Canada and abroad
- Develop a personal sense of responsibility for respecting and defending human rights
- Enhance their knowledge of the Internet and the use of the technology to further develop research and analytical skills.

BRAINSTORM

Before starting with a classroom discussion on the subject of human rights and refugees, have students work in teams to conduct some searches for information on the Internet to see what they may find (conventional sources may also be used). Have the student teams research the following: the Canadian Human Rights Foundation, United Nations High Commissioner for Refugees, The Canadian Council of Refugees, and Amnesty International. Perhaps each team might choose one organization, then summarize their findings in a brief report. What role do these organizations play in helping refugees and alleviating obstacles with regard to human rights abuses? What can the teams find out about the UDHR? How did it come into being? What were the circumstances? Who wrote it? Have each team summarize the relationship between human rights and refugees and incorporate it into their report. Have them present their findings to the class. (See Other Resources section for help and links in the research.)

The Universal Declaration of Human Rights contains 30 rights and freedoms. Of those, which would the class consider to be the most fundamental that must be respected at all times? Make a list on the board. Which are excluded and why?

Discuss the concept of asylum and what it means. How important is asylum to refugees? *Note:* Some members of the class may have direct experience with seeking asylum or may have been refugees at some point. Others may have family members who have experienced the same. With some degree of sensitivity, these class members may be encouraged to share their knowledge and experience with the others. They may wish to write their story rather than tell it. Please ensure they are comfortable with whatever process is chosen to share these stories with the class.

Choose five of the rights and freedoms listed in UDHR and discuss how they are applied (if they are), here in Canada. What difference do they make to the quality of life in this country? What if those rights and freedoms weren't respected? How would things change? Draw some conclusions and write them on the board. Create your own Charter of Rights and Freedoms for the class. Students can break off into teams and each team can write up their own based on the previous research and discussions that have taken place. Have the teams present their Charter to the class and compare them.

SPECIAL ACTIVITIES

Students will complete at least one of the following:

CASE STUDY #1

Olivia is 37 years old and she is originally from Chile. She came to Canada as a visitor and then decided to seek refugee status. In Chile, she was an organizer in a labour union that was at odds with the military-backed regime. Her friends and colleagues were thrown in prison. She received death threats. Olivia has an aunt and two cousins who live here. While here, Olivia had a child but did not marry. Her daughter is now three years old. Her application to be considered a refugee was refused. The board ruled that she must return to her point of origin and reapply from there. Since her daughter was born in Canada, however, she is allowed to stay. Olivia is appealing the decision.

- Does Olivia have a legitimate refugee claim? Describe the reasons why.
- Are Olivia's rights being violated? If so, in what way?
- Who is the real victim in this case?
- If Olivia must return to Chile, should she leave her daughter behind or take her along?

CASE STUDY #2

Mohammed is a 28-year-old Muslim from Bosnia. He and his wife and two children escaped the ethnic cleansing that eliminated most of the people from their village. Many of Mohammed's relatives and friends were killed in the conflict. Mohammed and his family made their way to Italy where they applied to come to Canada. Despite the fact that Mohammed is a trained electrical engineer and his wife is a schoolteacher, their application was rejected. Their youngest child has Down Syndrome. They were told by their case officer that, as a result of their child's condition, it is likely they would be a drain on the Canadian system and end up a ward of the state. Mohammed and his young family were turned away.

- Was Mohammed and his family treated fairly? Describe why or why not.
- Was the case officer discriminating against the family or merely doing his/her job?
- If the case officer was doing his/her job, then what has to change to eliminate any potential discrimination?
- Given the choice, should Mohammed proceed to Canada on his own and leave his family behind?

CASE STUDY #3

Anushka is 14 years old. She came to Canada from Armenia six months ago. She speaks some English, but not a great deal. She is going to a regular public school and is taking special classes in English to bring her skill levels up. Some of the students in school make fun of her. They ridicule her accent and the way she dresses. They think she is ignorant because she knows little of popular culture and things most of the others take for granted. They don't understand why she appears fearful and cries easily. Although her family is with her, their journey to Canada was long and difficult. Her family applied to come from overseas and, with the help of relatives who lived here already, their application was finally accepted. Anushka finds it difficult to make friends and although she feels physically safe, is still fearful of those in authority. It is a difficult adjustment for her in this new life.

- Is there anything that Anushka could do to ease her transition to life in Canada?
- Why are some students at school making fun of her? What do they gain by doing so?
- How can the environment at school be made more welcoming for Anushka and others like her?
- Are any of Anushka's rights and freedoms being violated as a result of the actions of some of the students at school? If so, list which ones.

RESEARCH ACTIVITIES

Students will complete at least two of the following:

1. Document the highs and lows of Canadian immigration policy during the 20th century. Some examples are as follows: the 1939 St. Louis passenger liner that carried 900 Jews fleeing Nazi persecution, the so-called "Ship of Fools," the incorporation of refugee definition into the Immigration Act, the Singh decision, Operation Shortstop, or the introduction of gender guidelines to the Immigration Review Board (IRB). What do these actions say about Canadian policy? What

was the follow-up? Was there any improvement or adjustments made to policy as a result? File a brief report.

2. What is the Message? The media shapes our perceptions to a large extent. Have the class monitor either the local newspaper, online news sites, or daily newscast for a period of a week. Have them select (or in the event of television, record or bookmark), the stories that cover refugees and immigration. Students will critically examine the coverage in those stories they've found. How are the subjects portrayed? What sort of language is used? What about images? What impression do the images convey? Students will write an analysis of the coverage they've discovered and determine whether the stories depict their subjects positively or not. If not, then how might the stories be written or shot to change the reader/viewer's perception of the subjects?

3. Refugee women and children make up over 80% of the world refugee population. The principle of family unity is of crucial importance to them. What makes this so important? What conditions contribute to underlining this importance to them? Research the human rights provisions that exist in international and national law that address this question. See the case studies above to further develop a case for family unity when it comes to refugees.

4. Select a country and research whether or not the government has ratified any human rights conventions, for example, the 1951 Convention Relating to the Status of Refugees, the Convention on the Elimination of All Forms of Discrimination against Women, the UN Convention against Torture and Other Cruel, Inhuman or Degrading Treatment or Punishment, or the Convention on the Rights of the Child. Does the government of the country selected live up to their international obligations in the treatment of women, children, and refugees? Do a search on the Internet. Check for articles and news reports coming out of the region. Develop a checklist of basic rights using the UDHR to measure how the country selected meets its responsibilities.

5. What is the difference between legitimate protest and "illegal" confrontation? Often it depends on how the state responds to the group that is protesting. Take a fictional group called the Pampoolians. They are concerned and upset about the conditions in the country of Pampoolia that operates as a military dictatorship where rights and freedoms are severely curtailed. A group of Pampoolians has staged a round of ongoing, peaceful protests in front of the Pampoolian embassy in Ottawa. How would the protests be viewed and dealt with here in Canada? Document actual examples of real protests to support your view. Contrast this with how you think the protesters might be treated if they staged the same in Pampoolia. What might happen? What rights and freedoms are protesters granted here? How might those rights and freedoms be violated in Pampoolia? Here too, document actual examples of protesters staging demonstrations in other countries and how were they treated. Write your report noting specifically the likely differences demonstrators might expect here in Canada as opposed to elsewhere.

6. Profile one of the following: Nellie McClung, Rick Hansen, Madeleine Parent, or Dorothy Nealy. How did each fight against some form of discrimination? Ultimately, what did they accomplish? Have their achievements been long-lasting, even affecting government policy? How important were these achievements?

CREATIVE ACTIVITIES

Students will complete at least one of the following:

1. Louis Riel led two armed insurgencies of Métis against the Canadian government. He was subsequently captured, tried, and then hanged. Despite the violence of their actions, the Métis had legitimate grievances against the Canadian government that weren't satisfactorily addressed. Write a one-act play based on the life and times of Louis Riel. Once the script has been written, put together a team of actors and technicians. Rehearse, then stage the play for other class members or classes within the school. What lessons can be learned from Riel's story? Are those lessons applicable today? Does the Riel story reflect the concerns of Aboriginal communities in Canada? If so, why?

2. Design a poster celebrating an upcoming anniversary of the Universal Declaration of Human Rights. How would you use the poster as a basis for a multimedia campaign aimed at getting the widest possible exposure? What other elements should be part of such a campaign? Who would you enlist to help you? What other media would you use? How would you fund it? Write a promotional strategy for your awareness campaign.

3. Choose a country and listen to some of its traditional music. Research the instruments and style of play. Is it possible to determine whether the music is used on formal occasions such as holidays or official celebrations? Or is the music more popular as a form of traditional folk music? Search for available music online, or see if there are any recordings available at the library. Students may have their own musical collections they can bring in. If feasible, write a song in that musical form about how it feels to be a refugee coming to Canada and starting a new life. Use the creative arts to explore new feelings and emotions. Perform the song for the class in any way that appears suitable.

4. You are a journalist covering an ongoing situation in Albania where native Albanians are subject to attack. Research the area and the history of the people who live there. What is at the root of the conflict? Why are the Albanians being attacked and who is attacking them? Write a series of news stories covering the unfolding series of events. Refer back to the media-related activity and be sure to incorporate the knowledge and information learned from that into this activity. Be aware of how the refugees in the story are portrayed and the sort of language used. Detail how the story should be illustrated or what photographs

are appropriate. File those stories to your "editor," the teacher. Has writing these stories changed the way you view regular media coverage of these issues and how might your perceptions be affected?

FINAL PROJECT

Have students select one of the following:

1. Design and create a class website, blog, or wiki page that focuses on refugees and human rights. Take the content and materials developed through the previous activities and post it on the site. Divide the class into teams and assign different areas for each team to research and develop. For example, one team may be responsible for content areas such as rights policies and conventions, case studies and so on. Another may be responsible for the design of the site, or social media feeds. If the class has an existing website, then this project can be set up as a special section of that site.

2. The Human Rights and Refugees Electronic Symposium. Using the 66th anniversary of UDHR as the starting point, organize an electronic symposium through the Internet with other schools in your community or across the country. You may want to extend the symposium to include schools from other countries around the world. Working in class, set the agenda for the symposium and based on the research done up to this point, look at the resources required. Consult the experts in the field. See Resource Section for names of organizations to contact. Decide on the time frame for the symposium. Will it take place on a single day or multiple days? Invite former and perhaps current refugees to participate in the symposium, allowing them the opportunity to help educate others about their situation and that of refugees. Create an event. Contact the local media to interest them in the symposium and invite them to cover it. Local multimedia or Internet companies may be co-opted to provide technical assistance and support. Involve parents and the community at large. Liaise with the local public library to draw on resources and to promote the symposium to their patrons.

RESOURCES

Films

The Burning Times
www.nfb.ca/film/burning_times

This documentary takes an in-depth look at the witch hunts that swept Europe just a few hundred years ago. False accusations and trials led to massive torture and burnings at the stake and ultimately to the destruction of an organic way of life. The film questions whether the widespread violence against women and the neglect of our environment today can be traced back to those times.

Carly
www.unhcr.ca/teachers/catalog.htm

Carly is an animated fantasy film that tells the story of a child seeking refuge and acceptance. Carly deals with themes such as cultural difference, exile, and tolerance.

Human Rights, Refugees, and UNHCR
www.unhcr.ca/teachers/catalog.htm

This package includes a video, posters, background information and unit plans, each containing a number of detailed lesson plans aimed at introducing refugee issues and how they are linked to human rights. The video is for secondary students.

Before Columbus
http://onf-nfb.gc.ca/en/our-collection/series/?ids=170302

Before Columbus is a series of three films, Invasion, Conversion, and Rebellion that describe, "with a few stories that stand for so many," the Indian experience in the Americas during the past five centuries.

Organizations and Publications

New Internationalist (Magazine)
Amnesty International
Refugee Update (Magazine)
Aboriginal Rights Coalition
Association for New Canadians
United Nations High Commissioner for Refugees
Immigration and Refugee Board of Canada
Canadian Council for Refugees
Inter-Church Committee for Refugees
Refugees in the Classroom

EPILOGUE

TEACH Magazine delivers hands-on tools and resources directly to teachers. This first volume of The Gold Book of Lesson Plans enables teachers to do what they do best; explore comprehensive themes with students creating a dynamic teaching and learning environment representing the best of 21st century education.

OTHER EDUCATIONAL PROJECTS FROM TEACH:

The Shadowed Road
An exploration of contemporary Ethiopia focusing on global citizenship, human rights, democracy and access to education.

www.theshadowedroad.com

The Ruptured Sky
An exploration of the War of 1812 from First Nations perspectives.

www.therupturedsky.com

80 Degrees North: The Canadian Arctic Expedition 1913–1918
An exploration of a dramatic but ill-fated exploration of Canada's north.

www.80degreesnorth.com

www.ingramcontent.com/pod-product-compliance
Lightning Source LLC
Chambersburg PA
CBHW042028150426

43198CB00003B/98